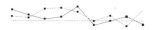

Say It with Data

ALA Editions purchases fund advocacy, awareness, and accreditation programs for library professionals worldwide.

SAY IT WITH DATA

A CONCISE GUIDE TO MAKING YOUR CASE AND GETTING RESULTS

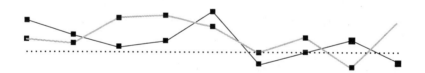

PRISCILLE DANDO

ala
editions

AN IMPRINT OF THE AMERICAN LIBRARY ASSOCIATION

CHICAGO 2014

Priscille Dando is a library information services educational specialist supporting the secondary library programs of Fairfax County Public Schools, Virginia. Her twenty-three-year career as a teacher and librarian has focused on best practices for instruction and advocacy for teens. She is a National Board Certified Teacher in Library Media and was named Teacher of the Year at Robert E. Lee High School in 2003. Dando earned her master's degree in library science at the Catholic University of America and is a member of the Young Adult Library Services Association (YALSA) Board of Directors. She serves on several advisory boards, including the National Forum on Teens and Libraries hosted by YALSA and supported by the Institute of Museum and Library Services.

© 2014 by the American Library Association.

Printed in the United States of America

18 17 16 15 14   5 4 3 2 1

Extensive effort has gone into ensuring the reliability of the information in this book; however, the publisher makes no warranty, express or implied, with respect to the material contained herein.

ISBNs: 978-0-8389-1194-5 (paper); 978-0-8389-9685-0 (PDF). For more information on digital formats, visit the ALA Store at alastore.ala.org and select eEditions.

Library of Congress Cataloging-in-Publication Data
Dando, Priscille.
  Say it with data : a concise guide to making your case and getting results / Priscille Dando.
     pages cm
  Includes bibliographical references and index.
  ISBN 978-0-8389-1194-5 (alk. paper)
  1. Communication in library administration. 2. Library statistics. 3. Libraries—Marketing. 4. Libraries—Evaluation—Statistical methods. 5. Library use studies. 6. Library surveys. I. Title.
  Z678.D17 2014
  025.1—dc23
                    2013020183

Cover design by Kimberly Thornton. Background photograph © Shutterstock, Inc. Type design by Mayfly Design in the Miller and Hypatia Sans Pro typefaces.

♾ This paper meets the requirements of ANSI/NISO Z39.48-1992 (Permanence of Paper).

Contents

Preface

For years school and public libraries have been facing critical challenges of sustainability and growth just as the nation at large has. For individual frontline librarians, it's easier to consider advocacy efforts to be someone else's job, but everyone has to own the responsibility of advocacy. For library program managers, the consequences have become too large to ignore the need for a sustained advocacy campaign. Being a frontline advocate requires vision, a deep understanding of the workings of the library, and a plan of relationship building and communication. Too often, the task seems so daunting, or the human and time resources so limited, that any effort to conduct deliberate, persuasive communication keeps getting pushed to the background. That's no longer an option. To be successful, all librarians should be invested in an ongoing plan of positive communication with stakeholders and decision makers in order to wield positive influence. Administrators, policy makers, legislators, and the public demand concrete, measurable evidence of need and success in order to support the library's mission. Communication is the foundation of advocacy, and effective communication is customized to a specific audience and strategically focused on a desired outcome. The essential question is, "What will ensure the biggest return for my efforts?" The answer? Data.

Some people break out in figurative hives at the mention of statistics, but any advocacy effort will be unsuccessful without them. Data-driven decisions may seem cold and detached, but personally I find that weighing the story that evidence communicates is a fair and sound process for making decisions. Mary Alice Anderson, now an online instructor in the School of Education at the University of Wisconsin–Stout, recalls how her diligence in recording usage statistics saved her middle school position as a media specialist. During a period when media specialists were being eliminated in her district, her principal was asked by the school board why he maintained staffing levels. He replied, "Five hundred kids a day, that's why."[1] Imagine a different outcome if Anderson hadn't kept and effectively communicated her data. While an emotional appeal is nearly always present in an advocacy campaign, it's the data, the evidence, that sparks a call for action. What humanizes it and makes it compelling is how it represents a story in context and creates a new understanding. The key is to tap into the story that numbers can tell. This book is intended to assist librarians and managers in school and public libraries in establishing communication through data as the heart of their advocacy strategy. Every librarian has a part to play in communicating an advocacy message; time invested in simple methods of communication will pay dividends.

I have found that a successful and influential communication plan includes four distinct elements:

1. A clearly defined objective paired with an understanding of target audiences
2. Compelling data at the heart of the message
3. Simple and arresting presentation of that data
4. Positive, persuasive communication techniques

These elements frame the basis of this book. And because integrity is critical throughout the process, I've also placed an emphasis on accuracy and validity in working with data and have advised on how to ensure both are present in your communication. I hope to reach not only those librarians who haven't had much experience in playing a role as an advocate for their programs but also those who are looking for a more systematic way to measure their success and communicate it effectively. I've taken a combination of research in the library, nonprofit, and business fields on these topics and examined it through my own experience as a self-appointed advocate for libraries. While a number of factors are always in play when working to influence others, I have found that if I plan my efforts around data as the core of my rationale for my objective, the results are consistently successful.

Why Is Using Data the Key to Success?

The stakes are higher than ever before when it comes to preserving and growing the success of library programs. Funders and policy makers are under pressure to make data-driven decisions. Unsubstantiated appeals to save or increase programs, staffing, and resources are almost never successful. A strong argument based on real data, however, can provide the leverage needed for a serious consideration of your proposal. In other words, in order for your message to be effective, you need to say it with data.

The first benefit of a data-based communication effort is the authority that comes with factual evidence. Data that speaks to your point is difficult to refute. You've put the time and research into providing measurable evidence that supports your objective; anyone who objects has the burden of countering that evidence in some way. Being prepared with easily accessible data inherently lends greater authority to you and your message. You are projecting confidence and knowledge, which encourages others to respect what you have to say. With sound data, you have preempted the tricky questions that most stakeholders and policy makers privately or openly ask: "How do I know that what you believe is true?" and "Why is this important to me?"

The second advantage of a data-driven message is its ability to tell an authentic story through numbers. Some data, of course, is qualitative rather than numeric. Qualitative data includes examples, testimony, descriptions, observations, and anecdotal evidence—for example, the opinions gathered at focus groups or in answers to open-ended survey questions. This kind of data is illustrative in a real-world sense, but presented alone it can be dismissed as evidence in isolation that does little to prove a trend or common experience. Pairing qualitative with quantitative data strengthens your message. Quantitative data is more along the lines of what we consider to be statistical and is most often expressed in numbers or percentages. Such data is often a measurement of some kind and can be used to identify trends, high and low values, or an overall count. And when you look at the numbers, alone or in combination with others, each one has a story behind it that is revealed by asking the question "Why?" It's a tricky thing to use statistics to determine the cause of something because there is rarely a simple answer. However, the process of digging deeper through the numbers can bring to light insights that speak volumes.

Here's a simple example. Suppose that, according to a tally of personal interactions at the information desk, the number of reference-related questions has been trending down sharply. This becomes a call to reduce staff because at first glance it seems as if fewer people are requiring assistance. The assumption is that patrons are taking advantage of search engines and other online resources and doing their own information retrieval. The library manager examining the bigger data picture sees, however, that the story behind the trend is more complicated. An analysis of usage data on all aspects of reference services shows a marked increase in e-mail and Twitter questions addressed to information desk staff. So the need for references services, rather than decreasing, has in fact shifted, as staff is required for answering reference questions not only in person but also virtually. While it would require additional research to determine if the availability of online reference help is the actual cause of the declining in-person interactions, the numbers justify the retention of library staff. If no data had been collected for online requests for assistance, this line of argument could not have been effectively deployed.

A third benefit of data-driven decision making, as we have just seen in the example of the reference desk, is that it can protect you against making incorrect assumptions. Under the influence of individual opinions and the "squeaky wheel" phenomenon, where you might feel obligated to a vocal minority, it's natural at times to take an assertion at face value and respond without determining if that assertion is accurate. If your advocacy campaign or communication plan is based on such an assertion, however, the objective could become skewed from reality, and ultimately, even successful advocacy efforts that meet the objective will miss the mark.

Here's a personal example. When I was a high school librarian, I worked with a large number of students who required individual help accessing information from one particular college-level database. These frequent interventions kept this database continuously on my radar, and I found myself recommending it to students with increasing frequency. I assumed the content must be helpful and that it was being used for assignments, but my evidence for this assumption was based only on my personal experiences with what seemed to be a large number of students. When it came time to look at my database subscriptions for the next year, I assumed renewing would be a no-brainer based on usage statistics, and in fact, I was primed to search for additional college-level databases because the demand for them seemed high. However, when I looked at the statistics provided by the vendor, I found that while there were a fair number of searches across that one database, the opening and downloading of articles was proportionately low. Checking on the statistics for other databases, I found that the majority of articles that were actually used were being obtained from solidly high school–level or easier databases. So while I was helping all those students with that one college-level database, even more students were using other databases independently, leaving me out of the loop. If I had requested increased funding for additional college-level resources, I would have been misguided. The moral of the story? Reliable, meaningful, and comprehensive data ensures that the requests you make on behalf of your library are based on real needs.

In the library world, generating statistics is nothing new. Libraries must constantly collect data as a measure of progress toward specified goals, to help make budgetary decisions, and to meet the requirements of grants and of state or district reports. But now, more than ever before, it is equally vital that libraries also leverage their data to document the value of their services and instruction.[2] I hope this book will serve as a primer for librarians looking to collect, analyze, and present data as part of a strategy for successful library advocacy.

Notes

1. Mary Alice Anderson, message to the author, September 23, 2012.
2. Sandra Nelson, "Presenting Data," in *The PLA Reader for Public Library Directors and Managers*, ed. Kathleen M. Hughes (New York: Neal-Schuman, 2009), 205–6.

Acknowledgments

Thank you to editor Stephanie Zvirin and ALA Editions for this opportunity. I am forever grateful to Pam Holley, Linda Braun, Angela Carstensen, and Vicki Emery for all their encouragement. My deepest gratitude goes to my family—Lynette Calcaterra, Kevin Dando, and Ellen Dando—for their love and support.

CHAPTER 1

Determining Need, Message, and Audience

Positive, proactive communication through evidence-based advocacy is a necessity for successful library programs. Often the most challenging aspect of any advocacy effort is determining the plan of action. Evidence-based advocacy without a systematic plan is likely to come up short on results. The communication effort rests on the effectiveness of the data in driving a clear, concise, and compelling rationale that triggers a desired response from an audience of one or many. Careful and strategic planning increases the odds of success. This chapter covers the first four of six steps that are essential to a successful advocacy message based on data:

1. Analyze your program to determine what it needs.
2. Articulate the desired objective that satisfies these needs.
3. Identify the appropriate audience(s) to help you meet your objective.
4. Determine the evidence that will resonate with your audience and connect to your objective.
5. Collect, analyze, and synthesize data to act as evidence.
6. Package and deliver the data as the core of your message, tailoring the presentation for your target audience(s).

The time and effort invested into the front end of this process will be returned in the form of positive results. The worst thing you can do is begin a communication effort without first systematically identifying its objectives and planning your strategy.

Analyze Your Program to Determine Its Needs

Because technology allows for collecting an enormous amount of statistical information, the temptation is to begin by reporting out all the readily available data. However, a look at the most effective advocacy efforts suggests that collecting data is one of the later steps in the process and that statistics must be reported strategically. Any strategy, of course, hinges on knowing what is needed and identifying a desired outcome to address it. Start the process by conducting a strength, weakness, opportunity, and threat (SWOT) analysis. What does the internal environment of your library program and the external environment of your public or school community look like?[1] Some questions to consider:

What are the assets of your program?

What areas need improvement?

How are most of your human and financial resources utilized?

What is an area of recent improvement or decline?

What avenues are open inside and outside the organization for positive growth?

What factors negatively influence the program?

Who are your avid supporters and detractors?

What is the priority of your parent organization?

How does your program compare with or differ from others nearby?

What positive and negative changes in your internal and external environment can you forecast for the near future?

This analysis is necessary as a way to crystallize your most pressing needs, and it cannot be done by a program manager in isolation. Determining which needs to target is crucial as it will drive all other steps in your communication plan. In some cases, creating a survey or focus group is an effective way to conduct the analysis and simultaneously gather some relevant data. (See chapters 4 and 5.) You might focus on the entire library program or on a single aspect, such as the use of technology. It's important to remember that this kind of advocacy is a continual process. There is no need to feel pressure to evaluate every aspect of your program and reach every audience all at once.[2] Determine a regular schedule for conducting the SWOT analysis. Waiting for a crisis before creating an advocacy plan is like searching for a flashlight when the power goes out only to find dead batteries. An ongoing advocacy program keeps policy makers informed, creates opportunities for building long-term positive relationships, and allows time for careful planning. Of course, unexpected developments will arise that force an immediate response. A lack of time is often a critical factor in these situations, and it limits the type of effective responses that are available.[3] What's most important is that the conclusions from any analysis be valid. They should be vetted by personnel inside the library program as well as by knowledgeable observers from outside.

The SWOT analysis may conclude that your library's needs are financial, policy related, or both. Financial issues can include budgets and funding for professional and paraprofessional personnel, programs, additional hours of operation, print and online resources, multimedia materials, equipment and equipment repair, professional development, support for special populations, furniture, renovation, marketing and outreach, hardware and software upgrades, and more. Nonfinancial needs may involve policy changes, reorganization, partnerships, operational guidelines, initiatives, and

directives from local, state, or federal government. You will need to
evaluate the following areas specific to school and public libraries
during your SWOT analysis:

Strengths or Weaknesses

Library staff
Organizational structure
Patron base
Support of community
Facility
Location
Technology
Print and online
   resources
Program offerings and
   services
Marketing or advocacy
   strategy
Online presence

Opportunities

Grants
Partnerships
Volunteer base
Community involvement
Business partners/
   sponsors
New initiatives
Strategic plan/School
   Improvement Plan

Threats

Budget cuts
New policy directives
Competing agencies
Increased costs
Bad publicity
New legislation

Determining needs may be a matter of deciding which ones are not
only most pressing but also likely to have solutions that you as an
advocate can adopt. In other words, the process of identifying needs
goes hand-in-hand with identifying a course of action or an objective that will address them. Remember to borrow on the library's
strengths and opportunities for leverage while considering how to
counter weaknesses and threats.

Articulate the Desired Objective

Grant Wiggins and Jay McTighe's work *Understanding by Design* has been a mainstay education model for developing effective learning opportunities in classrooms. Its main philosophy is for teachers to develop essential questions for a lesson and determine the desired outcomes before planning or embarking on lesson activities. Just as a teacher focuses first on the desired learning outcomes, so should effective communicators develop the objectives that will best meet their needs before considering any action. This *backwards design* concept allows you to tailor activities to achieve specific goals rather than develop a plan without context. Looking at an objective, a successful advocate asks the tough "why?" and "so what?" questions at the forefront because that is ultimately what will need to be done in answer to any critics.[4] Knowing the audience is the key to anticipating the right questions. Look to chapter 2, "Secrets of Effective Communication," for suggestions on building influential relationships.

As an advocate, it's never enough simply to bring awareness to a problem. Most problems have more than one solution. It's the advocate's job to consider all possible solutions and create a plan of action for implementing the most desired one. Present the solution to the problem to the stakeholder or policy maker in such a way that there can be no doubt about what you are asking them to do. Otherwise, you may get your audience to agree that outdated technology in the library, for example, is a pressing need, but then leave them with no clear idea of what action to take to alleviate the problem. Complaining about an issue is usually counterproductive. Keep energy focused instead on the desired outcome. Make sure that each data-based communication effort has an objective beyond simply informing. Be ready to articulate a targeted purpose with a tangible outcome.[5] Whether the goal is increased funding or a change in policy, this objective drives all aspects of a successful and dynamic advocacy effort.

Identify the Appropriate Audience

Savvy advocates understand the need to connect personally with an audience. Mark Smiciklas, a marketing strategist specializing in new media, defines a potential audience as "anyone who is influenced by your organization's information."[6] The medium of communication can be online or in person, spoken or written, but it has to tap into the interests and point of view of the intended audience. There is no such thing as a canned message that fits all audiences. Individuals inside and outside of your immediate environment will have different self-interests, concerns, and levels of prior knowledge on your issue. To make a difference, target and understand a specific audience, then meet its needs. Do the homework. Charisma influences an audience, but it can only go so far.[7] You are in charge of the data that is shared and how it is presented, and one of your most important challenges is to make your case meaningful to your target audience. Lila Herndon Vizzard is a researcher and evaluator whose career has revolved around the use of data in the decision-making process in the areas of maternal and public health. She recommends looking at your message from the audience's point of view and adjusting it accordingly. "If you're presenting to funders (or potential funders), then you need to be prepared to speak to efficiencies and return on investment. If you're talking to beneficiaries of services, you need to focus on impact. You also need to understand the data literacy of your audience. It's all about the story and what the data has to say to that particular audience."[8]

The first audience to identify consists of the individuals above and below your chain of command. If you supervise employees, it's just as important to include them in the process as it is to convince policy makers to act in your favor. Not only do your immediate colleagues have valuable insights into the needs of the library program and how to address them, they are also critical to the process of planning and conducting your advocacy effort. Involve stakeholders in the process from the beginning to encourage greater progress toward the objective and a greater commitment to data collection.[9] When thinking about your potential audiences, consider especially your supervisor's point of view and the perspective of that person's supervisor and so on, up to the ultimate authority over the organization. A branch manager, library director, principal, superintendent, library board, board of supervisors, or school board will require different approaches. Never forget to include your patrons—students, parents, PTA organizations, the public and surrounding community—as they will likely also require advocacy and communication efforts, and they each have a unique point of view. Remember, too, that there are many people who can speak on your behalf. Volunteers, program participants, students, book club members, parents, teachers, and regular visitors of all kinds have already demonstrated their interest in the library, and having them join you in your advocacy efforts can increase your authority with different audiences. And you can use Twitter, YouTube, Pinterest, Facebook, Tumblr, and other new media platforms to spread your message outside your library and, perhaps more importantly, to allow others to pass it on to an exponentially larger audience. Of course, you must prepare such messages in a way that makes it easy for supporters to promote them on their own. Providing compelling evidence in a clear and convincing way speaks to the audience and gets results. Look to chapter 2 for an exploration of how to connect with audiences.

Determine the Evidence

The most successful advocates provide a rationale for their request that goes beyond an emotional appeal. Presenting data gives authority to the speaker and substance to the request. Determining what evidence to collect can be a difficult decision because it involves a commitment of time and resources. The data should grab attention by communicating something that hasn't been heard before. Context is key. A novel presentation of statistics in a real-life context is the best approach.[10] Maintain a presence among the decision makers and think of what this audience would respond to. Anticipate questions and include that information in your presentation. What does this or any targeted group already know about your issue and what do they need?[11] Be prepared to stress how the stakeholder will benefit and be sure to be cognizant of the relevancy and urgency of your message—above all, don't waste anyone's time.[12] The American Library Association suggests some helpful questions to consider when crafting your message:

> What does your target audience know and think about your library right now?

> What do they need to know to help you reach your library's goal?

> What are the best ways to communicate with them?[13]

A financial board would be interested in the costs of any endeavor and would be most moved by a demonstration of how your proposal will save funds. Proposals that involve additional or reallocated money should include evidence that costs incurred will result in a valuable return to the program. If the audience is the school principal, evidence should be presented that outlines how your proposal assists in meeting the school's mission or supports a new initiative, or how it positively impacts student achievement, since those are generally the top priorities of school administrators. Focusing more specifically on high-stakes tests, achievement gaps, budget concerns, parent interests, and school image will also tap into what school administrators value.[14] Realize, however, that everyone has a unique frame of reference when processing information and that this will affect your audience's reaction to any given message. So while it is okay to make certain assumptions about an audience's interests and point of view, whenever possible test your message first to avoid misunderstandings.[15] Keeping the audience and objective at the forefront of the data collection process keeps the effort aligned for success.

A Simple Example

Suppose a SWOT analysis at a public library brings to light the large numbers of teens who arrive after school on weekdays. As a branch manager who sees both a threat and an opportunity, you need to determine the best way to respond. You decide that your objective will be to get special project funding for the creation of a designated teen space. Who are the people most invested in this issue, and who are the decision makers that can make your objective a reality? The likely audiences are all library staff, especially teen or youth services staff, teens that currently use the library and potential new users, the library director, the local Friends of the Library, and the library board. Perhaps grant providers and sponsors could be audiences, too. The message will be different for each audience, but once you've gained support from the other groups, the library board may be the ultimate audience and the group that will get things done. You could focus on the board's vision of providing dynamic services to special population groups, and your rationale should contain several data reference points and additional persuasive evidence. You could track the number of teens that come to the library on weekday afternoons over a specified period of time. If you also track the other groups of visitors, you'll have a much richer bank of information to report. Just giving the average number of teens visiting in a week may not spark much interest, but providing evidence that more teens come to the library between three and five on weekday afternoons than any other group of patrons has a better chance of grabbing attention. You may want to survey the teens themselves to see what they come to the library for, and how a designated teen space might be utilized and received by them. Refer to studies and statistics that show that designated spaces better serve this group, and explore other systems with branches similar to yours to demonstrate the need, prevalence, and value of these spaces. Tap youth organizations in your community for potential partnerships or for further information about options for teens in after-school settings. Before you present any of this information to the board, make sure to consult any available official guidelines. In this case, you would turn to YALSA for their National Teen Space Guidelines (www.ala .org/yalsa/guidelines/teenspaces) to see what is recommended and realistic for your situation. Flesh out any other details, such as level of support in the community for your project, changes that would be needed to the current physical arrangement of the library, any associated costs, and an implementation plan. Finally, develop strategies for presenting your evidence in the format that is best suited to your audience and most likely to successfully make your case.

The final two steps in the advocacy process—collecting, analyzing, and synthesizing data, then presenting it effectively—are explored in detail in chapters 3–6. But first we will explore the secrets of effective communication (chapter 2).

Notes

1. Lesley S. J. Farmer, "Marketing Principles: School Libraries and Beyond," in *Marketing Your Library: Tips and Tools That Work*, ed. Carol Smallwood, Vera Gubnitskaia, and Kerol Harrod (Jefferson, NC: McFarland, 2012), 33.
2. Ibid.
3. Sandra Nelson, "Library Communication," in *The PLA Reader for Public Library Directors and Managers*, ed. Kathleen M. Hughes (New York: Neal-Schuman, 2009), 172.
4. Grant Wiggins and Jay McTighe, *Understanding by Design*, 2nd ed. (Alexandria, VA: Association for Supervision and Curriculum Development, 2005), Gale Virtual Reference Library e-book, chap. 1.

5. John T. Warren and Deanna L. Fassett, *Communication: A Critical/Cultural Introduction* (Los Angeles: SAGE, 2011), 11.

6. Mark Smiciklas, *The Power of Infographics: Using Pictures to Communicate and Connect with Your Audiences* (Indianapolis: Que, 2012), Kindle e-book, chap. 5.

7. Jo Reichertz, "Communicative Power Is Power over Identity," *Communications: The European Journal of Communication Research* 36 (June 2011): 149, Academic OneFile.

8. Lila Herndon Vizzard, e-mail message to author, October 22, 2012.

9. Ibid.

10. Rueben Bronee, "Writing That Counts: Three Ways to Use Numbers Creatively to Communicate," *ContentWise*, January 2009, www.becontentwise.com/Article.php?art_num=5109.

11. Sandra Nelson, "Presenting Data," in Hughes, *The PLA Reader*, 206.

12. Janice Gilmore-See, *Simply Indispensable: An Action Guide for School Librarians* (Santa Barbara, CA: Libraries Unlimited, 2010), 99.

13. American Library Association, "Target Audience Planning for All Frontline Advocacy Staff," accessed January 21, 2013, www.ala.org/advocacy/advleg/advocacyuniversity/frontline_advocacy/frontline_public/goingdeeper/audienceplanning.

14. Gilmore-See, *Simply Indispensable*, 54.

15. Nelson, "Library Communication," 168.

CHAPTER 2

Secrets of Effective Communication

Analyzing data and understanding what your goals are in communicating it are not enough to guarantee success. Many elements contribute toward delivering a message that returns a desired result, and the first step is understanding the process of communication and the aspects that you do and do not have control over as the initiator of the communication. This chapter will discuss the overall strategies for successful communication and is not limited specifically to communicating data. The focus here is on communication that goes beyond simply being informative. In the world of advocacy, communication is all about influence. Your ultimate goal is to persuade someone else to agree with your message and to feel compelled to act in your favor. The medium doesn't matter—it could be in written form, delivered in a conversation or presentation, or communicated online—your goal as an advocacy leader is the same. Communicative power is transferring to your target the rationale and motivation that propels action on your behalf or on behalf of your interests.[1] An audience must be willing to engage with your communicative efforts, but ultimately you have the burden as the creator of the message to meet the expectations of the audience.[2] Unfortunately, there is no single strategy that guarantees success. Yet while there are no magic formulas, an understanding of the characteristics of successful communication can help you in shaping and delivering your message. Indeed, communication is a process, and for each person crafting a message or receiving one, it is likely to be a unique and complicated one.[3]

According to Warren and Fassett, "Communication is the collaborative construction and negotiation of meaning between the self and others as it occurs within cultural contexts."[4] The negotiation of meaning is critical. Just because you've delivered a message does not mean you've truly communicated it. Your recipients need to comprehend it as you intended, and for effective advocacy, they must be persuaded to agree with you and follow with action. Yet the challenge is that each person may approach your message from any one of a million different angles depending on an infinite number of variables. The delivery, your likability, and the environment play a part in how your effort is received. Additionally, the recipients' background knowledge, previous opinions on the topic, willingness to be open-minded, and sense of personal benefit play into their level of receptiveness. While some of these aspects are out of your control, there are many approaches to communication that research has shown can increase the probability of success.

Characteristics of Memorable and Effective Communication

Integrity of the Message

Speech coaches and public relations personnel may have tips for delivery, but the single most important contributor to the success of your communication transaction is the authority of the content. It is vital that the information included in your message be straightforward, clear, and accurate. An audience's receptiveness to any form of communication is based on a relationship of trust. One single mistake or inaccuracy can derail the entire message because it calls your credibility into question.[5] Therefore, the first priority is to vet the information you are conveying and pay particular attention to the data. Statistics are a common target for scrutiny. Because they are used as evidence to support a claim and taken as facts, they must be impeccable.

Comprehension

It may seem obvious, but the content of your message should meet the audience at its level of experience with the issue. Suppose a public library manager is looking for funding to hire a youth services librarian for her branch. Appeals may be made to the director of the library system for an endorsement, the library board for approval, and a state youth association for a grant. Each of these audiences will have a different level of familiarity with the work of youth librarians, and you will need to adjust the jargon, details, and evidence that you use in your message accordingly. If you speak above or below your target audience's level of comprehension, you risk turning them off. You will also want to repeat your key point: as a message is heard multiple times in multiple forms, it is much more likely to be retained.[6] Keeping it fresh is critical. Repeating the same canned message over and over is another way to alienate your audience. A teacher takes into account student learning styles; an effective communicator must take into account different listening styles and deliver the message in a variety of formats—visually, orally, and in written form. This accommodation to different formats makes it more likely that your audience will understand and retain your points.

Presentation

An open, appealing, and confident style of speaking greatly contributes to an audience's level of engagement and comprehension, just as simple and professional-looking graphics enhance visual attractiveness. There are general presentation guidelines for printed or online communications. Layouts must be appealing, clearly understandable, and presented in a logical manner. Because not everyone will take the time to read the entire message, choose carefully what you want to be read first. Focus on a balance of white space and text or graphics, remembering that a simple layout is most attractive. A solid block of text is going to be boring, merely skimmed or even ignored, so providing a narrative with some graphic representation is wise. Proofread carefully for spelling and grammar, but also for consistent spacing, font, and strategic use of color.[7] Chapter 6 explores the effective graphical presentation of data in more detail.

When you deliver your message in person, whether in conversation or as part of a presentation, your message won't be the only thing on display: you, too, will be judged by your audience. There are unspoken expectations for every environment, and while following them may not guarantee success, going against the norm will bring the audience's attention to you in a negative way. How you dress, the language that you use, how you sound, your gestures, and the way you move all contribute to the impression you make.[8] Particularly in face-to-face encounters, it is to the speaker's advantage to cultivate the most appealing manner to keep an audience engaged and receptive. Everything from your word choice and tone to the degree of formality you project plays a part in how others will react to your message.[9]

Presenting Yourself

There are strategies to keep in mind when preparing for a face-to-face encounter. These are recommended no matter the circumstances—a one-on-one conversation with a policy maker, a small group presentation, or a speech before a large audience. That age-old saying, "You only have one chance to make a first impression," is particularly important during encounters in which you want to favorably influence others. You have choices to make: dress professionally, be prompt, speak clearly and confidently, and know when to listen.[10] Your appearance and delivery will be judged along with the content of your message. The first rule is to not let your own insecurities or nervousness show. Exuding professional confidence (without arrogance) encourages respect and credibility. One way to further this impression is by focusing on your appearance. Dress for professional confidence and comfort. Whether deserved or not, our profession carries a stereotype based upon appearance. Dressing as a business professional in high-stakes interactions is recommended. It's better to be slightly overdressed than underdressed, but above all look neat and put together. If you are experiencing a crisis of confidence, consider your clothes to be your costume. You are entering a role, and if you act and look like the self-assured professional you want to be, no one will suspect your personal insecurities. Whatever your clothing, your body language communicates how you feel.[11] People tend to believe what they see. Is your stance communicating resistance? Or does your audience see positive engagement, with good posture and an open expression?[12] Try to gauge what kind of impression you are making. How does this compare to the impression you *want* to make? Most importantly, what impression will your target audience respond to most favorably? Read the body language messages your audience sends you as well. Crossed arms, furrowed brows, or tense expressions usually mean you need to adjust your approach.

Presenting that positive first impression in appearance and demeanor is critical, but the manner in which we communicate can't help but have an effect on how well we're received.[13] According to researchers Nikolaus Jackob, Thomas Roessing, and Thomas Petersen, verbal and nonverbal aspects of your speech make a significant contribution to the success of your communicative efforts: "Fluent speech is more credible than nonfluent speech."[14] Practice giving your presentation to eliminate verbal tics such as "uh," "um," "you know," and "like." Frequent pauses and a monotone voice can be so distracting (or sleep inducing) that it's difficult for others to recall the content afterwards. Vary pitch, volume, and tempo to keep the audience engaged. It's generally accepted that "a variety of vocal emphasis, gestures, and facial expressions will have the strongest possible persuasive effect on an audience."[15] Jackob et al. also believe that while content is the single most important factor, "audiences find speeches with vocal emphasis and/or with both vocal emphasis and the support of facial expressions and gestures, for example, more vivid, more powerful, more self-assured, and livelier."[16] Consider getting feedback from others. Your perception of yourself is not always how others see you. Watch video of yourself speaking and adjust as necessary. Being aware of the impression you are making is a continual process. As you are successful in your advocacy, you will continue to grow in confidence and build this impression for others.[17]

Building Relationships

As defined earlier, successful communication is not a one-way street. You can craft and present what you think is the most convincing message, but if your audience is not willing to hear and embrace it, you will fail to communicate. Relationships have a tremendous influence on communication. As researcher Jo Reichertz states, "It is always humans whose words have power; not words that have power."[18] In your role as an advocate, the balance of communicative power is often uneven. You seek to inspire another party, who may reject your appeal, to act in your favor. A figure of authority, such as a boss or police officer, has the greatest influence. Everyone knows the risks associated with ignoring the action such authority figures call for. Barring that kind of relationship, the most powerful catalyst for being open to communication is a feeling of mutual trust and credibility. Ensuring that your words and actions are consistent is the fastest way to develop trust. While building trust does take time, being aware that each interaction contributes to a relationship is key. As Reichertz observes, "With each act of communication, the persons involved contribute to the writing of a future open-ended history that will never be really deleted. Indeed, it will always influence the following communication processes."[19] Maintaining positive relationships with all stakeholders is simply good practice, as people have long memories when it comes to a bad impression. You never know when you may need to depend on any given relationship. Advocacy efforts are like bank transactions. There will be no cash to withdraw if you never make any deposits.

These relationships need to be in place before a crisis hits. Reach out and focus on being approachable to others to establish those first encounters that build a trusting relationship.[20] Another reason to build positive relationships is that the manner in which you are perceived has a strong influence on the level of credibility given to what you have to say. Greater stock is put into the opinions of people who are thought of as predictably reliable. Their messages are considered more substantial. Therefore, a high level of reliability when it comes to matching your words to your actions and presenting credible evidence along with your message builds a more powerful reputation and solidifies the positive relationships you are cultivating. Those that are not considered reliable will find themselves marginalized when they attempt to act as advocates.[21] A final and critical reason to focus on building relationships is that people are more likely to support something that matters to them. Finding common ground with someone is the easiest way to convince that person to act on your message. By establishing that connection early on in a relationship, you are much more likely to be taken seriously and listened to with an open mind.[22]

The Power of Persuasion

You've identified your audience and objectives, gathered evidence to support your proposal, and determined the content and method of your communication. Now it's time to put it all together. The organization of your argument and the format you use to present your evidence—orally or in written form—is best served by applying research-based persuasive strategies.

Offering a Message That Matters

Most messages contain an element of education. You are working to increase awareness on an issue in your library that is important to you. Simply transferring information is not enough, you need to make your audience care.[23] The key is to keep in mind that you are writing or speaking in order to connect with your audience. Humanize the message. Connect with their "needs, interests, and reservations."[24] It will be difficult to be influential if no one is affected by what you communicate.[25] Therefore, approach your content by seeking a relationship between your call to action and your target's self-interest. On the job, you can garner your boss's support by linking your objective to something *her* boss wants.[26] Speaking to a school or library board, focus on how your idea or need is imperative or appealing to *their* constituents. For example, when talking with your principal, demonstrate how your proposal fits into the School Improvement Plan. Your desired outcome and your audience's motivations should ideally share common ground. Link your message to important activities and initiatives in the overall organization in order to deliver on stakeholders' priorities.[27] Using this principle means there is no one-size-fits-all approach to getting what you want. Customize your message to meet the needs of different audiences. Assuming you have built and continued to foster positive relationships, understanding what would be mutually beneficial should not be a stretch.

Getting to "Yes"

Psychologist Kevin Dutton has researched and written about "split-second persuasion," namely how to convince someone to agree with you on the spot. Such an impulsive decision usually comes in response to an out-of-the ordinary encounter where a message is communicated in a simple but unexpected manner, often with humor. Dutton enumerates the elements of interaction that are present during these types of exchanges:

1. Simplicity: the message should be brief and uncomplicated—similar to the concept of an elevator speech. People tend to be biased toward simplicity.
2. Perceived self-interest: the proposal presented must have some identifiable benefit to the recipient.
3. Incongruity: the message should be unique in some way, and perhaps through the use of humor or some other element stand out from what is typically expected.
4. Confidence: the communicator should exude confidence and competence, so as to encourage trust.
5. Empathy: the message should be personal enough that the recipient has some emotional connection to the request and is compelled to assist.[28]

In addition to the scenario involved in split-second persuasion, Dutton's research has determined that with some foresight and strategy, the chances of being successful in any one-on-one negotiation can be significantly raised. He observes that politicians and advertisers have the simplest technique down cold for framing an argument advantageously.[29] The framing principle essentially states that controlling context influences meaning. In other words, the way the facts are framed can put a spin on interpretation. Set the context before getting to the main point.[30]

Let's say you're looking to fund additional databases. One of your high school's Improvement Plan objectives is to close the achievement gap and encourage minorities to take advanced academic courses. Approach your principal with the news that you have been investigating how the library program can support this goal and have come up with a plan of action. Present data indicating that the achievement gap begins to be most evident within the honors classes in the tenth-grade year, and that fewer minorities are enrolling in advanced courses in eleventh grade. Point out that tenth grade is when more independent and thesis-based research is taking place in English and social studies and that teachers report that finding and using appropriate evidence has been a greater challenge for struggling students. Make the case that by providing a greater variety of online sources where students can more easily obtain statistical information and scholarly articles, you will be able to more effectively teach the inquiry process of finding evidence to support a thesis. Since research assignments are a major component of both English and social studies courses during tenth grade, the instruction and use of these databases will enable a greater variety of students to perform at a higher level on assignments that can contribute positively to their overall grades and success. Provide a plan for collaborative instruction with the honors teachers that utilizes these additional resources and includes support for lower achieving students. (If they can join you in the meeting or endorse your plan, even better.) Finally, provide information about the databases you currently have and how these additional databases will strengthen the array of resources available. Include the cost. The focus in this scenario is not about getting the school to pay for additional databases but instead about showing how the library program actively contributes to student achievement and tapping into the principal's vested interest in implementing strategies that address School Improvement Plan objectives. "Preaching, lecturing, pleading, and bullying" turns people off emotionally, and you cannot make a "sale" that way.[31] Strategic framing, on the other hand, gives the argument greater weight—especially if the context is one respected by your target.[32]

Another commonly used principle in the art of persuasion is that of reciprocity. You may be familiar with the strategy of asking for more than what you need in the hopes that any necessary (or inevitable) compromise results in fulfilling the bottom line request as you intended. With reciprocity, each side is making concessions.

If an original proposal is rejected, and it's clear that the solicitor has made concessions for a smaller follow-up proposal, human nature encourages the person with the upper hand to acknowledge this and be more likely to accept the second offer out of fairness.[33] For example, you are looking to refresh the children's section to give it a more appealing, modern look. Your proposal is for new furniture and shelving, construction of a larger storytelling area, new carpeting, and new dedicated computers. If that proposal is rejected, follow up with a plan to repaint the walls, purchase new signage and a throw rug, and rearrange shelves to more effectively use the space. With a lower cost, this second plan has a higher chance of being accepted while still fulfilling the basic goal of refreshing the children's area. On the other hand, sometimes it is necessary to lowball an offer just to get it in the front door and begin a dialogue.[34] After having successfully completed a relatively simple proposal, a savvy librarian or manager can follow up with an additional one that takes the next logical step.

The urge to conform and confirmation bias can also be used to strengthen a rationale. Conformity is the idea that there is safety in numbers and outliers are taking a risk. Accordingly, most decision makers feel more secure in making a decision that appears to be going along with a group. Comparing your situation to others, then, is something to be considered when setting up your argument. If all the other middle schools in your district have full-time clerical help when yours is being cut, citing that comparison may make a difference. Principals are not usually looking to make decisions that set their school apart as something less than its competitors. While local comparisons are probably more powerful, you can also look to regional, state, and national data to tug on that tendency toward conformity. Confirmation bias is more difficult to get a handle on. It's the individual instinct to look at a situation and align yourself with the side that reinforces your previously held views. Countering previously established opinions is extremely difficult and cannot generally be accomplished by simply relying on the plain facts of a situation to speak for themselves. In order to counterbalance confirmation bias, you will need a preponderance of evidence that challenges previously held beliefs in order to be successfully persuasive.[35]

If what you seek at the end of a conversation is agreement with your position or a positive response to a call for action, do not forget the closing salvo. Without aggression but with confidence, phrase your request directly to elicit an answer. Do not word it in such a way that a verbal answer can be easily avoided. "Please support my initiative" leaves your request hanging, with no resolution in sight. How and when will you know if you have that support? A more direct "Will you support my initiative?" hopefully will gain an affirmative answer, but if not, it gives your audience an opportunity to air any remaining concerns about providing support. Finally, having your target verbalize a "yes" means that he or she will be more likely to follow through in order to be consistent.[36]

Constructing a Persuasive Argument

It makes little difference if a speaker is looking to persuade a group or an individual, the crafting of a successful argument must be done deliberately and with appropriate planning. An effective speaker must be able to tell a good story, and a coherent narrative is inherent to a persuasive conversation. For this reason, as we touched on above with the concept of framing, the order in which you present information tells an audience how to think.[37] There's never one single way to convey a message, and its content and delivery will depend on an understanding of the needs of your audience and how they intersect with your objectives. Still, there are some basic things to keep in mind when crafting a logical argument. First, consider the need for a thesis or claim that will be supported with evidence you provide.[38] Then verify your evidence—including both qualitative and quantitative data—against as many sources as you can. Your goal is to show a consistently high level of integrity of reasoning.

Your entire message is derailed if you are off track in even one element of your argument, so ensuring that there are no mistakes in your reasoning and that your evidence is sound is paramount.[39]

The Techniques of Reasoning

There are three common approaches to the order of an argument. Take a historical approach if the objective is to highlight trends and changes over time. Paint a chronological picture of the situation and conclude with today's circumstances. To justify shifting more funds to e-book purchases, you could do a simple run-through of circulation and online usage statistics over a period of time, showing the evolution in patron preference. Arguments arranged according to priority highlight the most important and compelling evidence first, then follow with supporting evidence and examples. Arguments incorporating a narrative logic lead the listener or reader to a logical conclusion by telling a story in context, with pieces of evidence gathered along the way, leading to a convincing conclusion.[40]

Philosopher and logician Stephen Toulmin developed a six-part model of persuasive argument: Claim, Grounds, Warrant, Backing, Qualifier, and Rebuttal. The most essential of these pieces are the first three. Claim is the thesis. (For example, more funds should be dedicated to acquiring books and resources in languages other than English.) Grounds are the evidence or data that supports that thesis. (Community demographics show a steady increase in Latino and Asian immigrants in the area, while library patron demographics do not show a proportionate increase for those groups.) Warrant is the connection between the claim and grounds. (Reaching out to Latino and Asian groups by purchasing materials in languages other than English will result in greater library usage by those groups.)[41] Making the warrant clear, understandable, and valid will bolster the strength of your argument. One of the most common errors is allowing an audience to see a disconnect between the evidence and the claim. A strategy to avoid that error is to decide whether to employ inductive or deductive reasoning. Inductive reasoning employs evidence in such a way that one piece leads to another, ending in a natural, or logical, conclusion. For deductive reasoning, you present the conclusion up front, then follow up with the evidence that supports it. With either approach, you need to illustrate the links between evidence and conclusion if you expect your argument to be successful.

Of course, there are a number of techniques used in building an argument that are generally ineffective and best avoided:

Slippery slope: claiming that if one action occurs, a whole string of other actions will occur.

Ad hominem attacks: questioning the person rather than the facts.

Straw person argument: setting up a counter argument that is easily refuted but that bears little resemblance to the actual opposition.

Non sequitur: distracting from a mistake or weakness by making an observation that is irrelevant.[42]

Successful communication is a result of tangible and intangible factors. The most important factor is the organization and content of the message. Making sure to consider how you will be perceived, your relationship (or lack of one) to your audience, and the motivating factors on both sides of the transaction also contribute to achieving the desired outcome. The librarian or program manager that takes these factors into consideration has a much greater chance of success.

Notes

1. Jo Reichertz, "Communicative Power Is Power Over Identity," *Communications: The European Journal of Communication Research* 36 (June 2011): 151–52, Academic OneFile.

2. Sandra Nelson, "Library Communication," in *The PLA Reader for Public Library Directors and Managers*, ed. Kathleen M. Hughes (New York: Neal-Schuman, 2009), 164.

3. John T. Warren and Deanna L. Fassett, *Communication: A Critical/Cultural Introduction* (Los Angeles: SAGE, 2011), 14.

4. Ibid., 7.

5. Sandra Nelson, "Presenting Data," in Hughes, *The PLA Reader*, 207.

6. Nelson, "Library Communication," 168.

7. Nelson, "Presenting Data," 209–14.

8. Warren and Fassett, *Communication*, 75.

9. Ibid., 34.

10. Ibid., 68.

11. Gloria Petersen, *The Art of Professional Connections: Seven Steps to Impressive Greetings and Confident Interactions* (Tucson, AZ: Wheatmark, 2011), 20.

12. Ibid., 21.

13. Nelson, "Library Communication," 164.

14. Nikolaus Jackob, Thomas Roessing, and Thomas Petersen, "The Effects of Verbal and Nonverbal Elements in Persuasive Communication: Findings from Two Multi-Method Experiments," *Communications: The European Journal of Communication Research* 36 (June 2011): 248, Academic OneFile.

15. Ibid., 251.

16. Ibid., 262.

17. Warren and Fassett, *Communication*, 67.

18. Reichertz, "Communicative Power," 162.

19. Ibid., 159.

20. Janice Gilmore-See, *Simply Indispensable: An Action Guide for School Librarians* (Santa Barbara, CA: Libraries Unlimited, 2010), 55.

21. Reichertz, "Communicative Power," 163–64.

22. Warren and Fassett, *Communication*, 196.

23. Ibid., 15.

24. Ibid., 33.

25. Nelson, "Library Communication," 164.

26. Kevin Dutton, *Split-Second Persuasion: The Ancient Art & New Science of Changing Minds* (Boston: Houghton Mifflin Harcourt, 2010), 166.

27. Gilmore-See, *Simply Indispensable*, 63.

28. Dutton, *Split-Second Persuasion*, 161–77.

29. Ibid., 107.

30. "Framing Principle," *ChangingMinds.org*, accessed January 11, 2013, http://changingminds.org/principles/framing.htm.

31. Dutton, *Split-Second Persuasion*, 113.

32. Reichertz, "Communicative Power," 148.

33. Dutton, *Split-Second Persuasion*, 114.

34. Ibid., 117.

35. Ibid., 133–39.

36. Ibid., 116.

37. Ibid., 101–2.

38. Warren and Fassett, *Communication*, 35.

39. Ibid., 53.

40. Nelson, "Presenting Data," 207–8.

41. "Toulmin's Argument Model," *ChangingMinds.org*, accessed January 11, 2013, http://changingminds.org/disciplines/argument/making_argument/toulmin.htm.

42. Warren and Fassett, *Communication*, 54–55.

CHAPTER 3

Working with the Power of Statistics

There are three kinds of lies: lies, damned lies, and statistics.

—Mark Twain

Few if any librarians entered the field thinking it was a great opportunity to learn how to use statistics. In fact, for many, statistics are a necessary evil, just something to insert into reports as part of a checklist of items to include. And it's true: without context, statistics are meaningless numbers. Library managers should never provide simple circulation statistics, website visit tallies, database hits, or other mainstays of library statistical reporting without providing the story behind them. Mark Twain did his part in encouraging a general suspicion regarding statistics with his famous quote. However, the noted Harvard statistician Frederick Mosteller offered a telling counterpoint: "It is easy to lie with statistics, but it is easier to lie without them." Whether you are making a case for change or for more funding, you need to be prepared to provide compelling evidence to support your rationale, and when gathered and communicated correctly, statistics are the strongest weapon in your arsenal—it's difficult to dispute hard facts.

According to David J. Hand, statistics are "the technology of extracting meaning from data," and the individual statistic should be a summary of some numerical fact.[1] It's the ability to gather *meaningful* statistics that separates those who use them effectively from those who simply gather and report numbers. The first step is to know the questions you need answered in order to craft an effective message. Then follow best practices to collect data that answers those questions accurately. It's arguable that the most important step is to interpret measurements and analyze them to the degree that a valid conclusion can be drawn (or so that equally valid new questions can be asked). Finally, package the statistics within your message in such a way that their significance is as clear as possible and your audience has what it needs in order to make a decision. As librarians, we've been trained to recognize the responsibility we have to report to the public and our stakeholders because of our need to be accountable.[2] Savvy library managers go one step further to ensure that data is not only used as a tool for improving the library program and services but also used strategically as a powerful tool for advocacy.

Considerations for Collecting and Interpreting Statistics

There's no doubt that wrangling with statistics can become a time-consuming exercise. Although time invested can result in powerful evidence, librarians need to determine the optimal balance between the energy devoted to collecting and analyzing statistics versus activities that are directly a part of running a quality library program.[3] To stay on target, always keep in mind the question, "Why are we doing this?"[4]

Any argument that includes statistics needs to put the numbers in context and explain their significance. Furthermore, statistics act as strong evidence only when they have been collected ethically, honestly, and without manipulation. Any measurements need to be consistently applied so that the resulting data can be considered accurate. Be prepared to explain your process for collecting statistics and to defend their validity. In some cases, it may be necessary to present the raw data along with an outline of analysis explaining how different conclusions were drawn. At a minimum, a precise description of what the data is measuring and how it was determined is critical to showing the authority behind a piece of evidence.[5] As the communicator, you have control over how the statistical information is presented. Resist any temptation to omit, oversimplify, or exaggerate data to shape it so it supports your message. Any challenge to your interpretation by someone who sees through those manipulations will be devastating to your integrity, eliminating any chance of success for your message.[6] Awareness of this tendency can make you a better judge when encountering statistics yourself. To take one example, consider this analysis, from a 2012 Bowker Market Research report: Fully 55% of buyers of works that publishers designate for kids aged 12 to 17—nicknamed YA books—are 18 or older, with the largest segment aged 30 to 44. Accounting for 28 percent of sales, these adults aren't just purchasing for others—when asked about the intended recipient, they report that 78 percent of the time they are purchasing books for their own reading.[7] What this statement doesn't present very clearly is that the majority of sales are by or for teens. In fact, while 55 percent of the buyers are 18 or older, they are purchasing less than a third of all YA books sold (the "28 percent" mentioned in passing). So the remaining 45 percent of buyers (presumably under 18) are purchasing more than three quarters of the books sold. Consider also that many young people are not buying books with their own money and the fact that the adults themselves report that they buy books for others (including teens), and this report has the potential to leave an exaggerated impression that adult readers are taking over the YA market.

To analyze large amounts of data, begin by determining the relationships between the numbers. The first step is to look at the distribution among the numbers. Is there a wide range between high and low numbers? Are the numbers spread out evenly within the range or clustered together?[8] An extreme value in the statistical spread or a change in statistics over time is an indicator that you need to examine any variables and determine why that happened. There may not be a clear-cut reason, but examining what doesn't fit the pattern can lead to a valuable insight or help to identify an invalid result.[9] Focus especially on subgroups of data—particularly in surveys. Is there a difference in response by gender, age, and so on? The million-dollar question is, "Why?"[10] That's when establishing a focus group might help to clarify results.

Suspicions regarding the use of statistics are probably rooted in the fact that the reporter of the data must be selective in how to analyze and report it. Take the use of averages. As a statistic, averages are valuable because they summarize a range of numbers into one representative number, and most people recognize averages as a common way to communicate a value. Of course, averages are generally unreliable if there is a small number set. And if there are extreme values on either or both ends (known as outliers), the average can be misleading. Less often used but sometimes more accurate in creating a picture of a range of data is the median. Whereas the mean is "a sort of central point balancing the sum of differences between it and the numbers in the set,"[11] the median is simply the "middle" number of a set—half of the numbers are above and half are below the median. Place the numbers in order from least to greatest and determine the middle number. This works fine when you have an odd number of figures. (Looking at a series of five numbers, the third number is the median, with two numbers below and two above.) When you have an even number of figures, find the two in the middle and determine their average. (With a series of six numbers, the third and fourth numbers are in the middle. You'll have to add them and divide by two to find the average and the true median value.) Finally, you may want to consider the mode—especially if there is a large number set. Mode is simply the most common value, the one that occurs most frequently.[12] For an explanation of mean, median, and mode, see table 3.1. For a comparison of the effect of extreme values, or outliers, on each, see figures 3.1–3.3.

Table 3.1

Mean, Median, and Mode Explained

Data set: 4, 17, 7, 5, 13, 17, 2, 7, 12, 20

Mean (average)	Median (middle)	Mode (most frequent)
Find the sum of all numbers and divide by the total number of figures.	Put the numbers in order from least to greatest. Determine the middle number. For an even set of numbers, find the middle two and calculate their mean.	Put the numbers in order from least to greatest. Determine if any numbers are repeated. If so, identify the most frequently occurring number(s). (If none repeat, there is no mode.)
4 + 17 + 7 + 5 + 13 + 17 + 2 + 7 + 12 + 20 = 104 104 ÷ 10 = 10.4	2, 4, 5, 7, 7, 12, 13, 17, 17, 20 7 and 12 are the middle numbers. 7 + 12 = 19 19 ÷ 2 = 9.5	2, 4, 5, 7, 7, 12, 13, 17, 17, 20 7 and 17 both occur twice.
The mean is 10.4.	The median is 9.5.	The mode values are 7 and 17.

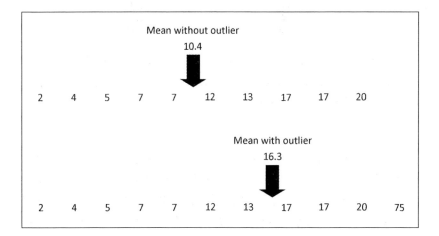

Figure 3.1. The mean, or average, is more influenced than median or mode by outliers—or the less typical results (in this case, 75 is an outlier). Compare figures 3.2 and 3.3.

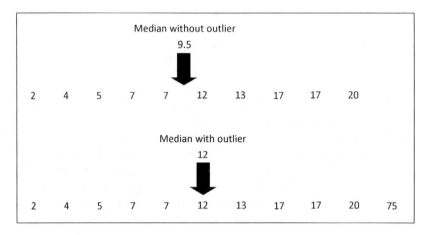

Figure 3.2. The median, or middle number, is only slightly influenced by the outlier. Compare figures 3.1 and 3.3.

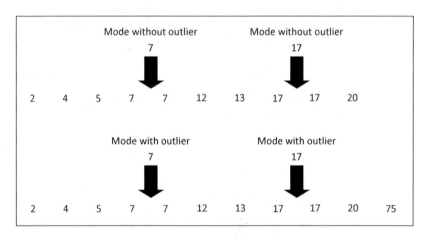

Figure 3.3. The mode, or most frequently occurring number (or numbers), is not influenced by the outlier. Compare figures 3.1 and 3.2.

So let's say that you want to create an analysis of the number of walk-ups to the information desk with the purpose of determining any need for a change in the schedule or to add additional staffing. You want to analyze one month's patterns. You instruct the staff on how to record interactions and how to mark the different types—for example, reference questions (help with locating and using resources, readers' advisory, and the like) or questions that are mainly directional (locating the bathroom, signing up for a children's program, or fixing the printer, to name a few). You'll want to break your results down in a number of ways, looking for trends or anomalies. Start by examining the timing of the reference questions by week, day, and time of day. Does a pattern emerge? Continue to sort by type of assistance required and see if categories can be established by clustering results.

Protecting the Validity of Data Interpretation

Undetected human or technical errors can alter results so that the interpretation of data leads to an inaccurate conclusion. Ethically, it is imperative that conclusions are drawn using valid results. Therefore, it's critical to be aware of situations that can skew results. Incomplete data is a common occurrence. If some observations or measurements are missing or were not collected, it is difficult to project a data sample that is accurate for a generalized conclusion.[13] In building an argument, it is important to identify and account for any missing data and to determine why it is incomplete. In practical terms, however, there are few options for re-creating missing data because faulty assumptions could be made in trying to fill the gap. It's much better to be diligent when planning for and collecting data so that the problem of missing data can be avoided when recording or measuring information in the first place.[14]

Inaccurate data will also lead to a faulty conclusion during a statistical analysis. Many circumstances can lead you astray, including human error in transcribing measurements, inconsistent methods of collecting information, misunderstandings of definitions, and calculation errors. Looking for outliers in a number range or for data that seems largely disproportionate may help in detecting errors, but determining the cause of such discrepancies may take more work. Be suspicious of results that suddenly change in spite of consistent variables.[15]

Collecting Local Statistics for a Proposal

Just because you have the ability to collect statistics on one or more aspects of the library program doesn't mean they will be useful to you in an advocacy sense. Some internal statistics are useful because they can inform you, for example, on which databases show the heaviest use and must be renewed, or what days of the week are busiest for walk-ins and require more desk coverage. For the audience outside of the library staff, however, those numbers may not mean much. It is crucial, therefore, that you identify your audience and pair their needs with your objectives. This is the only way to determine what type of statistical gathering would be most effective to use as evidence in a rationale.

Remember, too, that you don't have to conduct or rely on a long-term, complicated study to make statistics work for you. One simple example is a school librarian whose objective is to convince the principal to fund an upgrade in ten computers. The librarian might first strive to answer the following questions:

Why is there a critical need for a computer upgrade?

How are the computers currently performing?

Is the current situation negatively affecting students? If so, in what way?

Why is upgrading computers the best solution to this problem?

An argument can be made fairly easily without using statistics. Here is what such a rationale might look like as part of a written proposal:

Currently, the library is experiencing a critical need to upgrade ten of twenty-six computers included in the library alcove. These computers are the oldest ones in the library, and at this time, they are not performing well enough to support students' needs for completing research and assignments. They take an inordinate amount of time to log on to the network, and they crash when graphics-heavy documents are accessed. They are not able to play video without freezing. Students cannot easily access the library databases, especially the multimedia aspects of them. The overall slowness is very frustrating to students, and they often will leave the library if these slower computers are the only ones available. Teachers are reluctant to book the alcove space because more than a third of the class will be on these lower functioning machines and will not be as productive. Because a full-capacity memory upgrade was purchased three years ago, the only viable solution for this problem is to acquire new computers. The overall cost for ten new CPUs is approximately $7,000.

In some cases, that might be enough to get approval for the purchase; a more effective message, however, would address the concerns of the principal as well. For example, the principal might have the following priorities (in no particular order):

To meet the instructional needs of all students and staff in the school.

To manage a limited budget by using funds most effectively.

To ensure technology is used to foster student achievement.

Strengthening the argument to meet the principal's achievement-oriented and budget-conscious priorities, could involve measuring computer performance and describing the negative effects of the older computers in quantitative terms. So, taking one to two weeks to evaluate the situation, the librarian could do the following:

Include a survey sheet on a clipboard at all computer terminals and ask students to record how long it takes for the computers to log in and what they were using the computers for; leave space for any additional comments about the computer's performance.

Determine how old the computers are compared to those in the rest of the library and the rest of the school.

Tally how many times each computer has crashed in a given time period.

Determine the percentage of students who use the library. Some schools have a computer sign-in tied to their student information system: students simply type in their ID number as they enter the library, and the program records each student visit in a database. This system makes it easy to calculate the percentage of the student body that uses the library.

A revised statement for the proposal blending the principal's priorities with statistical evidence might look like this:

Currently, the library is experiencing a critical need to upgrade ten of twenty-six computers included in the library alcove. These computers were acquired seven years ago and are the oldest ones in the library—the library's other computers are 3–5 years old. According to the school inventory, the average age of all computers in the building is 4.5 years, making these ten computers among the oldest in the building. At this time, they are not performing well enough to support students' needs for completing research and assignments. For the past week, students have been self-reporting their computer log in times, and these ten computers take an average of twelve minutes each to connect to the network, more than 47 percent longer than the newer library computers. They tend to crash when graphics-heavy documents are accessed and are not able to play video without freezing; in the past week, each computer has had to be restarted a minimum of four times a day. Students cannot easily access the library databases, especially the multimedia aspects of them. The overall slowness is very frustrating to students, and they often will leave the library without completing their task if these slower computers are the only ones available. Teachers are reluctant to book the alcove space because more than a third of the class will be on these lower functioning machines and will not be as productive. Because a full-capacity memory upgrade was purchased three years ago, the only viable solution for this problem is to acquire new computers. The overall cost for 10 new CPUs is approximately $7,000.

Use of Outside Statistics

The purpose of incorporating national, state, or regional statistics is to draw a comparison to your local situation. If your situation compares favorably with the outside data, that is an opportunity to show how well you are doing when compared to others and validates what is happening in your library. If your data is less favorable than national or state findings, then it can be the basis for an argument for more funding or changes in policy to keep up with the standard set by similar libraries elsewhere. Saint Marys Area Middle School librarian Ellen Stolarski found success with this technique. As part of a grant process, she used a rubric and local statistics from her library to measure how her collection fares against state recommendations. Seeing the data fall short of state recommendations opened the door to a problem-solving conversation with her principal, and successfully demonstrated the need for an additional half-time aide.[16]

There are plentiful resources that provide library statistics on a state and national level, and these may be helpful in your local advocacy efforts. Most famously in the school community, there's the national School Libraries Count! survey run annually by the American Association of School Librarians (AASL). The survey covers staff activities, hours and staffing, collection size, technology, visits, and expenditures.[17] Coming out of the Colorado State Library is LRS, or Library Research Service (www.lrs.org), which collects data and research on school, public, and academic libraries. This resource also contains valuable survey results, impact studies, and a variety of statistics both historical and contemporary, on a state and national level. The Pew Charitable Trusts (www.pewtrusts.org) is a well-respected organization that produces reports and press releases on a wide range of topics. As part of its mission, it "applies a rigorous, analytical approach to improve public policy, inform the public, and stimulate civic life." Of course that includes regularly publishing studies involving all types of libraries. An impressive collection of online resources for librarians looking for statistics is provided by the Researching Librarian (www.researchinglibrarian.com/stats.htm), which not only points you to additional websites that collect or report on library statistics but also recommends sources for learning more about working with statistics. Another good place to go is the ResourceShelf (www.resourceshelf.com). Though not strictly limited to library statistics, the ResourceShelf is a useful collection of research, education, and technology reports and includes both a blog and an e-mail newsletter of highlights from the week.

Being able to measure the success and needs of your library program is critical to successfully communicating with stakeholders and others outside of your program. With some planning, a strategic plan for collecting data can pay off in a multitude of ways. Keeping a balance between what is meaningful, reliable, and easily collected is the key to feeling comfortable with statistics and confident in applying them to your advocacy message.

Notes

1. David J. Hand, *Statistics: A Brief Insight* (New York: Sterling, 2008), 4.
2. Adam Holland, "The Stat Factor," *Library Journal* 133 (August 1, 2008): 50, General OneFile.
3. Ibid.
4. Mathias Weyland, "The Wise Use of Statistics in a Library-Oriented Environment," *Code4Lib Journal* 6 (March 2009), http://journal.code4lib.org/articles/1275.
5. Hand, *Statistics*, 13.
6. Lila Herndon Vizzard, e-mail message to author, October 22, 2012.
7. "Young Adult Books Attract Growing Numbers of Adult Fans," Bowker, September 13, 2012, www.bowker.com/en-US/about us/press_room/2012/pr_09132012.shtml.
8. Hand, *Statistics*, 37–38.
9. Weyland, "Wise Use of Statistics."
10. James Cox and Keni Brayton Cox, *Your Opinion, Please! How to Build the Best Questionnaires in the Field of Education*, 2nd ed. (Thousand Oaks, CA: Corwin Press, 2008), 56.
11. Hand, *Statistics*, 39–44.
12. Ibid., 44.
13. Ibid., 54.
14. Ibid., 61.
15. Ibid., 61–64.
16. Ellen Stolarski, e-mail message to author, September 23, 2012.
17. "School Libraries Count!," American Association of School Librarians, 2012, www.ala.org/aasl/researchandstatistics/slc survey/slcsurvey.

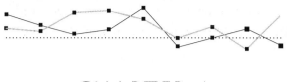

CHAPTER 4

Methods of Measurement: Surveys

No matter the form, surveys are "based on the desire to collect information (usually by a questionnaire) from a sample of respondents from a well-defined population."[1] Probably the most common form for gathering data in the past five years has been the online survey. With the popularity of SurveyMonkey, Google Forms, and other free or subscription services, it's a simple process to distribute a survey to hundreds if not thousands of people and receive real-time responses. Surveys conducted by telephone, by mail, on paper, or in person, while often more expensive and time-consuming, also have their uses. There is a huge body of research devoted to survey methodologies, and developing a survey that will give quality results relevant to your ultimate objectives takes strategic thought and planning. Ultimately, considering cost, timeliness, available human resources, efficiency of distribution, and analysis of results should make the best method clear for each situation. Looking at those criteria, online surveys would seem to be the go-to option, but in some situations it might be beneficial to try another method or a combination of methods.

Mail

Surveys conducted by traditional mail are becoming rare because of the cost involved for delivering and returning them, the low completion and return rate, and the length of time required before results can be analyzed. Although an older clientele may be more comfortable with a paper survey, these considerations usually ensure that the traditional mail option is off the table.

Telephone

As of 2005, surveys were still most commonly administered by telephone.[2] While some people might be more likely to respond if they are talking to a live person, for others the timing of the call and the general annoyance factor related to unsolicited calls may negate any advantage. Although surveys are exempt from the Do Not Call registry,[3] the general public may be unaware of that and react negatively. An even more important consideration is the increase of wireless-only households with no traditional landline. According to a 2010 report of the American Association for Public Opinion Research, upwards of 25 percent of all households receive phone calls solely through cell phones, and among young people aged 18 to 34, the percentage is even higher—so much so that the association considers surveys limited to landlines only and including this age group to be unreliable.[4] The cost of acquiring random landline and cell phone numbers or having an agency conduct the survey is substantial. Of course, depending on the purpose of the survey, you may already have access to the phone numbers—particularly if you are polling only patrons with library records or parents of students enrolled in school. Should you decide to conduct a telephone survey, interviews should be brief and simple, with no question longer than about twenty words.[5] A final consideration is the consistency of the interviewer asking the questions and human error in recording or coding responses. All interviewers should be trained to deliver the questions in the same manner and should understand the need to be diligent in recording answers accurately.

Paper

Paper surveys can be a good choice when you want immediate feedback. For example, a paper survey completed on the spot by a visitor to the library will generate information that is immediate and perhaps related to the current visit. This feedback can be followed up with a telephone or online survey, or even an invitation to participate in a focus group. It is difficult to get a large number of surveys completed in this manner, however, and of course the pool of applicants is narrowed to only those who walk through the door and have the time and inclination to answer the questions. This precludes the results from being generalized to the overall population. Still, keeping the purpose of the survey in mind, it may be beneficial to combine paper surveys with other methods since this is a way to catch respondents who may not be available by phone or online. Keep in mind that collecting, scoring, and coding responses will take significant time with this method. Another possibility for getting on-site feedback is to have a computer terminal set up with access to an online form or survey, or to train library staff to conduct brief interviews and record the verbal responses.

Online

Thanks to their relatively small cost and ability to reach a large number of people, instant results, flexibility, and ease with which data can be sorted and interpreted—not to mention the option to add graphics and audiovisual material—web-based surveys have become the most popular choice for library branches and schools. One of the greatest advantages is the ability to drill down responses very precisely through the "skip pattern" option within most online survey programs.[6] For example, if a respondent answers that she is a regular visitor, to a question about frequency of library use, the program can skip questions geared toward determining reasons why someone does *not* use the library and redirect the questioning to focus on the top reasons for visiting. By customizing each survey according to the characteristics and previous answers of each respondent, you essentially have the ability to administer more than one survey at a time. While the advantages are obvious, it's important to be aware of some critical disadvantages when using online surveys. The most pressing potential problem is that the sample group may be biased. Since only those who have Internet access or feel comfortable sharing information online are likely to respond, the results will reflect the views of that demographic and may not be applicable to the population that does not have access to technology or a level of comfort with it. And be aware that technical difficulties with links or software can cause problems in the administration of online surveys and that online data must be kept secure.[7]

Survey Process

As described in chapter 1, "Determining Need, Message, and Audience," the use of backwards design as a planning principle should apply to any program of measurement or assessment. The first step is always to determine what the desired outcome is, followed by how you intend to report that outcome.[8] Applying this principle to surveys means deciding what you want to know about a population before designing the questionnaire or determining whom to survey. Surveys can be used for a multitude of purposes, from assessing areas for improvement and determining prevailing points of view to gathering data to help in decision making. In addition to what the administrator of the survey learns, an overlooked benefit of conducting a survey is that it communicates to those who complete it that their opinions are valued.[9] Using the results in advocacy efforts, however, requires additional foresight. An essential question is, "What do we ultimately want to communicate with the results of this survey?" Surveys are a powerful way to demonstrate to policy makers the value of the library to patrons, the specific resources, services, and programs that are valued the most, and how library offerings directly affect the community inside and outside of the library.

After determining why the survey is being conducted and what you hope to learn from the results, the next step is to determine who you need to answer the questions. A target population must be explicitly defined based on demographics and geography. Look to the goals of the survey to logically decide on participants.[10] But before beginning the process of choosing respondents, make sure that you have identified available funds, time, and human resources so they can be allocated appropriately, and decide on the survey method. Draft questions on the topics that will elicit responses relevant to the survey goals. And make sure to allocate time for testing the questions in advance, by administering the survey to a handful of library or school staff, including yourself. Note any areas of confusion or concern that might need revision.

A special consideration when preparing any survey is to include the non-English-speaking members of your target group. A 2001 report by the National Institute on Aging and the National Institute of Child Health and Human Development, *Diverse Voices: The Inclusion of Language-Minority Populations in National Studies*, provides guidelines for including this population. Cost is often cited as a barrier to reaching out to language-minority groups. However, there is a significant threat to the validity of the survey if the sample does not include representative groups, and any costs incurred are necessary to the integrity of the process. Particularly with school and public library services, English-language learners may be a critical needs group that benefits significantly from library programs. Make every effort to include non-English speakers in the sample and to obtain professional translations of your survey. Many school districts and local governments are staffed to provide such a service. Having bilingual staff members available to answer questions or concerns about the survey is helpful as well. Use of bilingual community members may also be an option, but be aware that quality control of the translation or presentation of the survey may be compromised. And while websites offering machine translations may be tempting to use, they are not generally as accurate as professional translators and the results must be carefully vetted before being accepted.[11] (For a checklist of things to consider, see appendix A.)

Sample Size

Sample size and composition are important variables in ensuring that the results of your survey can be generalized to the population as a whole and therefore be considered valid. The larger the sample size the better, especially if you are generalizing to a diverse population. For small groups (the senior class or, for a small school, the entire student body; all teachers; and in a small branch all library card holders) it is generally better to conduct a census. A census surveys every possible person in a population rather than a representative group, which is considered a sample.[12] In determining a sample, keep in mind that the integrity of the answers depends on the sample being random.[13]

At a minimum there must be a purely random procedure where each person has an equal chance of being chosen, but for more precision, a stratified random sample can be used. In this scenario, the population is divided into demographic groups. Then within each group a random sample is determined. This ensures different groups with different points of view are represented. If you develop a proportionate stratified random sample, each demographic group has the same ratio of participants. In a disproportionate stratified random sample, the ratio of each group echoes that of the population at large.[14] Best practice entails drawing a sample that is truly representative of the overall population targeted.[15]

There are a variety of complicated formulas that help calculate the optimum sample size. Thankfully, online sample size calculators, such as the one offered by Creative Research Systems (www.surveysystem.com/sscalc.htm), can help. No matter how the sample size is calculated, there are three factors in play—confidence level, confidence interval, and response rate. Confidence level reflects how confident you are that a group within the survey would give the same answer if asked the question again. An acceptable rate is 95 percent. Confidence interval is also known as margin of error. This is the percentage point range up or down from a given result that the answers would be reflected among the larger population. Response rate refers to the percentage of individuals exposed to the survey who actually complete and submit it. This of course is difficult to predict and is not included in most sample size calculations. Once you know you need a certain number of responses, you should adjust for the predicted response rate so the final tally of participants is within a valid sample size.[16] For example, let's say that your school population is 1,700 students. After locating a sample size calculator, you input 95 percent confidence level with a 4-point confidence interval. The result is a need for 444 respondents in order to be able to generalize results to the total student population. However, you predict only a 60 percent response rate. In order for a 60 percent response rate to yield 444 completed surveys, the survey must be distributed to at least 740 students (60 percent of 740 is 444).

Survey Design

First impressions are everything in a survey, and increasing the odds that it will be completed and submitted is a priority in survey design. Don't overlook the obvious, such as making sure your survey is as professional looking and attractive as possible. According to Don Dillman, whose "tailored design method" is a staple of survey research, the elements of social exchange theory come into play when designing a survey. It's critical that the participant trust the authorship and organization behind the survey.[17] Establish this through a carefully written introduction that discloses the purpose of the survey and how the results will be shared, ensuring anonymity when possible. (Make sure you understand the difference between anonymity and confidentiality. An anonymous survey is one in which the administrators cannot determine which individual provided which answer. In a confidential one, the administrators can match a participant with an answer for the purpose of internal analysis but will not disclose identifying information to anyone else.)[18] Identify who is conducting the survey and any sponsors involved. Describe why it is important. If people recognize the value of the survey, they are more inclined to take part.[19] Another recommendation is to provide a reward for participation. This could be as simple as a thank you for completing the survey, a link to real-time results, or even a small, tangible reward such as a coupon for reduction of a late fee. Above all else, the emotional response the questions generate will influence whether it is completed. The questions must not feel condescending, the information should not be too personal or embarrassing, and answering the questions must never be inconvenient or difficult.[20] See appendixes D–G at the back of this book for some sample surveys.

Question Options

There are a number of decisions to make that will help your survey be successful before crafting actual questions. Is there a need to compare this survey's results with the results of past surveys? If so, care should be given to repeat the questions asked in the previous surveys and duplicate the process as closely as possible.[21] Consider carefully the order of the questions. (Most people who abandon a survey do so after the introduction or the first few questions.)[22] It's critical that the first question be interesting, relevant, and easy to answer. Be aware of the "halo effect": there can be an unintended carryover from one question to another, which then has an effect on subsequent answers.[23] Here are some tips for structuring your survey to increase the odds that it will be completed:

> **Use a descriptive title.** Titles that contain the word "questionnaire" or "survey" may turn some people off.[24] A title like "Student Voices Count! Reflections on the Hammond High School Library Experience," on the other hand, comes across as inclusive and encouraging.

> **Start with easy questions.** This gets the momentum going and is less likely to trigger the kind of head-scratching

pauses that could cause the respondent to abandon the survey as too difficult to answer or taking too much time.

Group questions by topic. Providing headings for topic areas shows professional organization and prevents needless repetition.

Pose the most substantial questions after the easier ones, but leave difficult or sensitive questions for last. The longer a person spends on the survey, the more likely he or she is to complete it, so you do not want to turn someone off early on in the process. Still, you'll want to put your most important questions toward the front so that they have a better chance of being answered, even by those who may feel the survey is too long. This is a delicate balance to achieve, and testing your survey with a pilot group before administering it officially will help determine if the questions are in the optimal order.

Gather demographic information at the end. Asking personal information up front may discourage some from continuing with the survey. Establish trust and get responses to important questions first before asking questions about gender, ethnicity, and so on.

Limit the number of open-ended questions. Because they are more difficult to answer and inherently take more time, it's better to use open-ended questions sparingly and only for a specific purpose.[25]

Crafting Questions

The success or failure of any survey depends mostly on the design of the questions. There are a multitude of considerations, and different options will work for different goals and circumstances. Regardless of the type of question, it should be worded as clearly as possible. Use simple vocabulary and choose fewer words—questions should be written at the expertise level of participants and should avoid professional jargon.[26] That said, all questions should be understood in the same manner by everyone who reads them, regardless of their experience. Ferret out any unintentional meanings when testing the survey.[27] Another concern is the validity of the questions. You do not want to word them in a leading manner that would steer answers in a certain direction.[28] For example:

> Because most of the library's computers are six years old and are
> not capable of handling streaming video, they should be upgraded.
> ❑ Agree   ❑ Disagree   ❑ Neutral

This is a leading question because the setup makes it highly likely that respondents would agree with the statement. They may not have the entire picture, however. Perhaps the vast majority of the computer use is for simple Internet searching and word processing, which the older computers handle fine, and there are enough newer computers to meet streaming video needs. There certainly is a case for upgrading older computers in this situation, but the wording of the question is too subjective. A better question would be this one:

> The library computers meet my needs for assignments.
> ❑ Agree   ❑ Disagree   ❑ Neutral

Including an optional comment field with the question can clarify the results.

Avoid the common mistake of creating a "double-barreled" question—one that actually is measuring two elements at once.[29] For example, the question "Please rate the importance of computers and online databases to your library experience" has a major flaw. Perhaps the patron uses the computers to access e-mail, websites, or printing, but doesn't use (or know about) the databases at all.

There is no way to accurately answer that question, and it should be divided into two separate ones.

Closed vs. Open-Ended Questions

The most basic decision to make when creating a question is if it will be open-ended or closed. Open-ended questions allow for respondents to generate their answers freely in their own expressive way:

> In what ways has visiting the library after school helped you complete assignments?

Closed questions force respondents to choose from a menu of answers:

> In which of the following ways has visiting the library after school helped you complete assignments?
> - ❏ Use of computers
> - ❏ Meeting a tutor, study group, or classmate
> - ❏ Getting assistance from the library staff
> - ❏ Use of library resources
> - ❏ Taking advantage of uninterrupted time

Closed questions are generally considered more reliable because the results can be quantified, and there is no need to try to interpret a respondent's intended meaning as there is with open-ended questions.[30] However, greater care is necessary to craft a closed question so that the multiple-choice options or the rating-scale elements cover all possibilities without being too lengthy.[31] One way to cover all the bases is to include an "other" category, By requiring an explanation, "other" provides an open-ended contingency for those who don't see an accurate answer among the options. Including a "not applicable" (n/a) option can help ensure the accuracy of closed questions as well. If "other" or "n/a" is not included and, as with many online surveys, the reader is required to answer every question, the data may become invalid or the survey abandoned if an appropriate choice for each individual hasn't been included.[32]

Closed questions generally involve either multiple-choice or scaled responses. A rating scale has a range of answers expressed numerically (choose a rating from 1–5) or with descriptive terms (choose a rating from poor, fair, good, excellent). A Likert item uses a rating of the level of agreement with a statement (strongly agree, agree, disagree, strongly disagree). Decide whether a neutral response is desirable. Rating scales with an odd number of choices will have a middle option that is neither positive nor negative (the 3 on a 1–5 scale). Be aware that some people will gravitate toward a neutral option because it doesn't require much thought, and that such answers tend to count less in the final analysis.[33]

Don't forget to identify any screening questions that might prove helpful. Demographics are important, but there may be other considerations depending on the situation.[34] For example, in a school-based survey, you may want to know how long a student has been enrolled at the school. Someone who has been there less than thirty days may have an incomplete experience with the library, and those answers may not be indicative of the larger population.

Perhaps the best test of an effective survey question is to ask yourself, "Is this question necessary to address the survey objectives? Is it clear, concise, and unbiased? Can participants answer the question accurately?" When you can answer all of those in the affirmative, it's time to pilot the survey, make adjustments, and administer.

Interpreting and Reporting Survey Results

If possible, input data on a spreadsheet in order to look at it in different ways. First, look for obviously inappropriate or implausible responses—these do not need to be included in the report—but be careful not to unduly manipulate the results. Take the time to look for trends by comparing the answers of different subgroups and, if you have data from previous surveys, any similarities or differences in results. It's best to convert data into percentages. This is the easiest way for others to understand results and for you to draw conclusions. With closed questions in particular, don't forget to look at averages and high and low responses as well.[35] See appendix H for an example of how you might go about analyzing a survey question.

Dealing with Nonresponses

Nonresponses refer to those questions that have been skipped by respondents who have otherwise completed the entire survey. In online surveys, it is possible to force an answer to any or all questions. Be careful about forcing answers, however, as anyone who really does not want to answer a particular question may then be forced to abandon the survey.[36] The critical decision to make is whether or not to include nonrespondents in the percentages of answers. In other words, if you have 1,000 people who completed the survey, and only 800 answered a given question, then you need to either calculate your percentage out of the 1,000 people who were exposed to the question or the 800 that actually answered it. Whichever you decide, the most ethical thing to do is to disclose the method of calculation and identify how many people (or what percentage) were nonrespondents. (For example, 53 percent, or 273 out of 514 who answered the question, disagree that the computers in the library are meeting their needs; 6 percent of total respondents did not answer the question.) If you decide to include only those who responded, be aware that this limits your sample size and may make the question invalid for generalizing to the larger population.[37] Finally, consider following up with those who failed to respond to the survey in a different mode of communication from the original invitation. Send an e-mail, try a phone call, or even send a postcard—whichever seems most appropriate—to encourage participation.[38]

Determining Validity of Results

It would be unethical to report results you knew to be invalid—that's why careful planning and testing of the survey, before it is administered, is so critical. You will want to scrutinize both the process and the results to anticipate any problems with the survey that you or others may identify.[39] Once the actual survey has been administered and the results are in, it's too late to alter them. Before reporting results, ensure their validity by considering the following elements:

Did enough people respond to the survey? Did you determine your minimum sample size, and did the number of actual respondents equal that number or greater? Are there certain underrepresented subgroups that you may need to try to contact by different means?

Did most respondents answer all questions? When a significant number of people skip a given question, that's an indication that something is wrong with the question itself and that it should be discarded.

Is there a reasonable variety of responses to each question? If an overwhelming number of people answered a multiple-choice question with the same answer, it could be that most people feel that way, or it could be the result of a leading question.

Is there a suspiciously high number of "not applicable" or "other" answers? In this case, either too many of the questions are less than clear or the respondents were not the most appropriate target for the survey, as the questions did not seem relevant to them.[40]

Reporting Results

Survey results should be reported and shared in a clear and concise manner—visuals are recommended. (See chapter 6, "Presenting Data to Get Results," for a discussion on data visualization and making the greatest impact.) It's good practice to share results not only with your target audience for advocacy but with the survey respondents themselves. Your report should highlight the goals of the survey, and it should be customized to the audience you wish to reach. The level of detail and vocabulary should meet your audience's level of familiarity with library operations and best practices. One of the simplest and most organized ways to share results is to repeat the original questions and list results underneath. After synthesizing all the data, however, you may decide that organizing by theme, strongest to weakest response, or actionable items will be more effective. Craft an introduction that puts the survey in context.[41] The American Association for Public Opinion Research offers best practice recommendations for reporting survey results. Briefly stated, the report should include the following:

- A description of who sponsored the survey and who conducted it.
- Its purpose and objectives.
- A copy of the survey or a list of questions administered.
- A definition of the sample used and the procedure for obtaining it. The sample size should be disclosed.
- An explanation of the completion rate and any trends regarding nonrespondents.
- How overall conclusions have been determined.[42]

The raw results should always be available so others can draw their own conclusions and verify yours. When you are presenting the results of your survey as part of an advocacy effort, there are some additional considerations to keep in mind. As we saw in chapter 3, data is not especially meaningful without context. In order to be compelling and persuasive, your survey results report must "tell the story" behind the numbers. Add the narrative necessary to summarize the meaning and implications of the results. Draw the logical line between the results and how they act as evidence in support of your desired outcome. This must be done in a clear, direct, and convincing way. Stretch the truth or make questionable connections and you weaken your case. Reflect back to your objective for the survey and the essential, overarching questions you hoped the survey would answer. Those ideas should provide the framework for your report, not just a summary of the results. Having said this, no one will be won over by an overlong report. Filter down to the main idea—brevity is a virtue.[43]

Library surveys are not a new concept, yet many fail to use the results to their greatest potential as an advocacy tool. There is a tremendous advantage in knowing how to develop, administer, and analyze a survey and then report on the results so that they act as powerful persuaders in a targeted communication campaign.

Notes

1. Ronald Czaja and Johnny Blair, *Designing Surveys: A Guide to Decisions and Procedures*, 2nd ed. (Thousand Oaks, CA: Pine Forge Press, 2005), 3.
2. Ibid., 45.
3. "Is Survey Research Covered by the Do Not Call Rules?," American Association for Public Opinion Research, accessed January 14, 2013, www.aapor.org/Is_Survey_Research_Covered_by_the_Do_Not_Call_Rules_1.htm.
4. AAPOR Cell Phone Task Force, *New Considerations for Survey Researchers When Planning and Conducting RDD Telephone Surveys in the U.S. with Respondents Reached via Cell Phone*

Numbers, American Association for Public Opinion Research, 2010, www.aapor.org/Content/aapor/AdvocacyandInitiatives/ Reports/CellPhoneTaskForceReport/.

5. Czaja and Blair, *Designing Surveys*, 48.

6. Ibid., 41.

7. Alicia Williams and Nancy Protheroe, *How to Conduct Survey Research: A Guide for Schools* (Alexandria, VA: Educational Research Service, 2008), 68.

8. Ibid., 74.

9. Ibid., 3–4.

10. Czaja and Blair, *Designing Surveys*, 3, 14.

11. *Diverse Voices: The Inclusion of Language-Minority Populations in National Studies: Challenges and Opportunities*, ed. Rose Maria Li, Peggy McCardle, Rebecca L. Clark, Kevin Kinsella, and Daniel Berch, prepared by National Institute on Aging and National Institute of Child Health and Human Development (Bethesda, MD: 2001), www.nichd.nih.gov/ publications/pubs/upload/Diverse_Voices.pdf.

12. Williams and Protheroe, *Survey Research*, 24–31.

13. American Association for Public Opinion Research, "Best Practices for Survey Research," accessed January 17, 2013, www.aapor.org/Best_Practices1.htm.

14. Williams and Protheroe, *Survey Research*, 40–41.

15. Margaret E. Ross, "Surveys and Survey Results," in *Encyclopedia of Educational Leadership and Administration*, ed. Fenwick W. English (Thousand Oaks, CA: SAGE, 2006), Gale Virtual Reference Library e-book.

16. Ibid., 37.

17. Don A. Dillman, Jolene D. Smyth, and Leah Melani Christian, *Internet, Mail, and Mixed-Mode Surveys: The Tailored Design Method*, 3rd ed. (Hoboken, NJ: Wiley & Sons, 2009), 22–23.

18. James Cox and Keni Brayton Cox, *Your Opinion, Please! How to Build the Best Questionnaires in the Field of Education*, 2nd ed. (Thousand Oaks, CA: Corwin Press, 2008), 74.

19. Czaja and Blair, *Designing Surveys*, 90.

20. Mack C. Shelley, "Questionnaires," in English, *Encyclopedia of Educational Leadership and Administration*.

21. Czaja and Blair, *Designing Surveys*, 70.

22. Ibid., 94.

23. Shelley, "Questionnaires."

24. Cox and Cox, *Your Opinion Please!*, 44.

25. Williams and Protheroe, *Survey Research*, 93–95.

26. Shelley, "Questionnaires."

27. Czaja and Blair, *Designing Surveys*, 6.

28. Ibid., 72.

29. Shelley, "Questionnaires."

30. Czaja and Blair, *Designing Surveys*, 13.

31. Williams and Protheroe, *Survey Research*, 92.

32. Chris Dubreuil, "Greater Insight: The Online Dimension," *Marketing*, July 28, 2010, 13, General OneFile.

33. Shelley, "Questionnaires."

34. Czaja and Blair, *Designing Surveys*, 71.

35. Williams and Protheroe, *Survey Research*, 102–4.

36. Czaja and Blair, *Designing Surveys*, 44.

37. Williams and Protheroe, *Survey Research*, 105.

38. Cox and Cox, *Your Opinion Please!*, 47.

39. Ibid., 119.

40. Ibid., 96.

41. Ibid., 111–15.

42. AAPOR, "Best Practices for Survey Research."

43. Cox and Cox, *Your Opinion Please!*, 59.

CHAPTER 5

Methods of Measurement: Focus Groups

While data is often considered in the form of quantitative statistics, qualitative information is a critical ingredient in communicating the story behind the numbers. Comments on surveys can provide some additional details about the participants' points of view, but to truly get a feel for specific feedback, to be able to follow up on answers and drill down to a more meaningful level, focus groups are well worth the time. Considered de rigueur for movie marketing and political campaigns, focus groups are usually employed to gather feedback on an existing product or service or to test something new.[1] Certainly, focus groups can play that important role for any library, but there is also a powerful opportunity to gather testimony to communicate with policy makers and the public through a carefully conducted focus group.

Advantages and Drawbacks to Focus Groups

Different disciplines have their own take on the use of focus groups—there are competing and complementary recommendations in the literature from the respective disciplines of psychology, marketing, sociology, and communication. Essentially, focus groups are a category of group interview in which data is collected from a targeted cross-section of the population, usually with a common identity.[2]

A focus on patron satisfaction, expectations, needs, and habits cer-tainly will help a library manager and staff improve services. How-ever, using that same information to defend budgets, staff positions, policy changes, and the like can be just the approach that your library needs as it looks to protect valuable services or address areas for improvement. Being able to directly quote participants and report specific user experiences and impressions carries a lot of weight. Not only will the focus group results help to determine unmet needs, but they will also provide the leverage necessary to make a successful campaign for funds and policy changes.

There are some drawbacks to using focus groups. It takes a signif-icant amount of time to prepare for the event, conduct the discussion, and transcribe and analyze the results (and it's usually beneficial to hold more than one focus group with varying demographic profiles). And it's a relatively small number of people who will be providing their views—it could be a mistake to make major decisions based on a few isolated conversational experiences. The group will only be as successful as the moderator is skilled and prepared. Of course a professional can be hired, but in many cases it will be up to a staff member to conduct the session, and those with little experience may find it a difficult task. Still, these challenges are not insurmountable, and the rewards can be significant. What's the difference between a focus group and getting feedback through open-ended questions in a survey? As James and Keni Brayton Cox describe it, "Questionnaires collect less information from more people. With interviews, you typi-cally obtain more information from fewer people."[3] Put another way, surveys provide shallow feedback with a broader reach while focus groups provide deeper feedback from a limited pool.

Creating a Focus Group: Considerations

As with all data-gathering techniques, the very first consideration is determining exactly what you want to measure and what the desired outcome of a focus group would be. Why are you conducting it? What information can be determined from a focus group that would be difficult to obtain through other methods? Do you have access to recent survey results? What did you learn there that you can follow up on during the focus group interview? Don't determine this alone. Include the entire staff or collaborate with colleagues in other locations to brainstorm what to measure in order to broaden your point of view and benefit from a fresh perspective. (For a checklist of things to consider, see appendix B.)

Choosing Participants

Identifying your goals and objectives in conducting the focus group will not only help steer the creation of questions but also give insight into who should be invited to participate. For example, if you are looking to justify increased expenditures for subscription databases, feedback from users would be more beneficial than the opinions of nonusers. In a school setting, you'll have to consider the main three groups—students, parents, and staff—when choosing participants. Within these, there are some ready-made groups that have the potential to provide meaningful feedback. These include the Student Government Association (SGA), class officers, parent-teacher organizations, and the school leadership team.[4] The public library may have a Teen Advisory Group (TAG), Friends organization, or library board to pull from. Still, best practices would argue for including a mixture of fans and users of the library, on the one hand, and those you would like to see increase their library participation, on the other.[5] Group dynamics should be a priority consideration. A successful focus group experience can depend on "intrapersonal factors and individual differences, interpersonal factors, and environmental factors."[6] If participants don't feel comfortable enough to respond to questions honestly, the results of the focus group may end up being unusable. While to a certain degree it is the responsibility of the moderator to make sure everyone feels at ease and participates equally, there are some negative tendencies within groups that can be avoided by bringing together the right combination of individuals. Be aware of differences such as age, gender, ethnicity, experience with the topics, and personal familiarity with the moderator. For people to feel most comfortable with each other, they should be able to relate to one another. For adult groups, aim for similar socioeconomic factors. For children and teens, group by age bracket.[7] While there is debate about the optimum number of people to include in any one focus group, most sources indicate that six to ten participants is an appropriate number. As all these factors related to group dynamics should make clear, it is recommended that more than one focus group is held before drawing significant conclusions or making decisions based on results.[8]

Ensuring a Comfortable Environment

The goal of the moderator should be to provide a stress-free experience that participants enjoy while encouraging a lively discussion.[9] Setting the scene is an important step. The first priority should be comfort—pay attention to lighting, temperature, individual space, noise, and a pleasant aesthetic free of distractions. The most comfortable seating arrangement is around a table with plenty of space where everyone can see each other. Table tents with participants' names on them will reduce the awkwardness of not knowing each person. Providing lunch if you can will ensure no one feels hungry or thirsty and may on its own provide an incentive for both young people and adults to participate.[10] The overall atmosphere should be relaxed and informal, and don't forget to make the actual location and appointment time convenient for participants.[11]

Crafting the Questions

There are two types of interviews: very scripted, with a strict and inflexible wording and order, and "semi-structured," where there are predetermined questions, but they lend themselves to more of a conversational format.[12] The second, less structured option seems more helpful because it gives the group the opportunity to react to each other's comments and can lead to some conclusions that the organizers may not have anticipated. A focus group session should last from sixty to ninety minutes, and that will require a minimum of six questions, allowing everyone to participate, respond to each other, and give the moderator an opportunity to summarize the main points at the conclusion of each question. The questions themselves should be planned very carefully. Consider asking a team to come together to brainstorm. Have the team work independently then share their ideas with the group to be evaluated for inclusion by everyone.[13] Each question should clearly relate to the predetermined goals and objectives. There should be no doubt what information you are seeking with each question and why it is being included.[14] A helpful technique is to role play the draft questions ahead of time to hear how they sound. This verifies that the questions are clear and concise, and that they target the desired information.[15] Once the final questions have been determined, you might consider sharing them with the participants ahead of time to give them an opportunity to reflect on their answers, but that is not a requirement for obtaining thoughtful responses.[16]

As a rule, questions should start with a general focus and then move to become more specific.[17] Karen Becker, a business consultant and president of Becker Associates, has advice for developing focus group questions. Although her target audience is the business world, these tips are easily adaptable to public and school library settings. Broad-based, general questions can start with words like *Describe, What,* and *Tell me.* More focused questions often begin with *How, Should, Is, Who, When,* and *Where.* Becker provides many sample questions which can be modified for a library-related focus group. Some questions are looking for positive, reinforcing comments while others are looking for feedback for improvement. Here are some examples, modified for the library setting:

In what ways does our library perform well?

What are the best features of our resources?

What aspects of our services/resources would you strongly recommend we *not* change?

What are the top two to three issues that are important to you related to the library?

Looking into the future, how do you see your library needs evolving?

What resources or services do not perform well?

What situations do you find awkward or difficult when using the library, its services or resources?

In what areas can we improve our relation with patrons (students/staff/parents)?

If you had a magic wand, what would you change about our resources and services?[18]

It's important to pose questions that indicate both what the library is doing well and what needs improvement. Positive responses can be used to validate specific resources and services and justify maintaining them. Look at the negative responses not as criticism but as leverage to argue for a policy change or additional funding to fill a gap or improve offerings—you now have concrete evidence of the need.

Conducting a Focus Group: Procedure

After determining objectives, testing questions, and choosing participants, there are still a few tasks to complete ahead of the event. Since the desirable size is six to ten people per session, send about eight to fifteen initial invitations to ensure there is an adequate number—and keep sending additional ones if necessary. The invitation should of course include the basic logistical information about time, length, and location. It should also include information about the purpose and objectives of the focus group, how the information will be used, and why their feedback is important to you and the library.[19] Describe any incentives you are offering for participation, and don't forget to mention you'll be providing lunch or other refreshments. Follow up with those that don't RSVP, and remember to send a reminder the day before the session.

Structure of the Discussion

The indicators of a successful focus group are a relaxed session where everyone feels comfortable and willing to share their views, no one dominates the conversation, and there is a "group cohesiveness" that keeps the momentum going.[20] The moderator's job is to ensure the smoothness of the session and to keep the discussion on track in order to elicit a meaningful conversation. There should be another staff person who is responsible for recording information and assisting in the process. Getting the data correctly recorded is paramount, and many focus group planners choose to create an audio or video recording of the session. Be sure to notify participants ahead of time. It's also necessary to assure them that specific responses will not be attributed to individuals without their permission.[21] Any additional observers should be kept to a minimum, as their presence may make it harder for participants to relax. After introducing yourself and other staff members attending the session, and welcoming everyone and making sure all are comfortable, the agenda should be straightforward. Start with an outline of what will occur during the session, explaining the goals for the focus group. Recite any ground rules and explain the method of recording, then have everyone introduce themselves briefly. Warm up with some general questions and then move to more specific ones, each time summarizing the main points before moving on to the next question. Leave room in the agenda for any necessary breaks. When all questions have been answered, bring closure to the session, thank everyone for coming, and offer to provide a copy of the report.[22]

Moderator Tips

Moderators are discussion facilitators, not hardball interviewers. Yes, they must ask probing questions, but always in a nonthreatening or nonjudgmental way. Participants should feel at ease throughout the process and leave feeling positive about participating. During the actual discussion, the moderator's task is to ensure that everyone is included, that the group stays focused on the questions, and that what is being recorded is an accurate interpretation of their views.[23] Being organized and prepared cannot be overemphasized.

One of the most valuable skills of a moderator is the ability to actively listen and follow up on answers on the spot.[24] At times it will be necessary to prompt for greater detail.[25] Be aware, however, of any one person monopolizing the conversation or exhibiting behavior that may intimidate or otherwise influence the group.[26] Several strategies can counter this. Start a round-robin approach after a question, giving everyone a chance to express their views. Simply calling on a specific person to begin answering the next question can move the conversation away from a monopolizer. A generally effective technique is to ask the group to write down answers to questions before opening the discussion. That way everyone expresses their personal views without undue influence, and the conversation can move along faster as speakers don't have to ponder their answers when called upon.[27]

Keep in mind that the moderator should not respond to any comments with more than curiosity. It's critical that answers be honestly offered, not influenced by the subtle or not so subtle reactions of the moderator. This is particularly important when negative comments are expressed. A focus group is not the time to take criticism personally—consider it an opportunity to learn and to work toward improvement.[28] Sometimes a negative comment will lead to a too-detailed description of recommendations. A key point for the entire discussion is that you are seeking information on what the library is doing well and what it needs to do better—and why. You are not looking for solutions to a problem. That is something the library staff can study and determine. Instead of allowing the conversation to stall on recommendations, ask "What will having that do for you?" to get to the crux of the issue.[29] It can be helpful to quantify the issues that are being raised by the group. For example, during a break, have the staff member who is observing and recording create a chart that lists the needs and other issues identified to that point. After the break have the participants individually write a ranking of 1–5 reflecting the importance of each item. Then ask them to rate how well the library is meeting those needs or addressing those issues using the same 1–5 scale.[30]

Bring closure to the session by asking for any final comments. Summarize the main points of discussion, and provide everyone with an opportunity to contribute any additional ideas in writing.[31] Giving them a brief evaluation sheet to complete could elicit comments about issues that the questions didn't address or that participants would feel more comfortable writing than expressing in front of the group. Sending a follow-up thank you note with a copy of the final report is a thoughtful gesture.

Analyzing Focus Group Outcomes

Immediately after the session, the moderator and observer should make notes independently on the main outcomes of the session. Make observations on the relative success of the session as well as on the content of the feedback. Notes on participation level, body language, disruptions, and surprises will be helpful in assessing the process.[32] The next step is to review the transcript or recording and draw conclusions. Organize comments into categories and look for patterns, trends, and relationships among the answers.[33] Revisit the original objectives for the focus group and evaluate how successful the session was at meeting them. This immediate post-group analysis should be conducted independently by the moderator and the observer then later compared to reconcile any differences in perception. They should work together to create a summary report. While there's no standardized form, a report should be presented in such a way that it communicates the facts of the session, including date, location, number of participants, names of moderator and observer, the goals and objectives of the group, and the original questions asked. Conclusions should be categorized according to theme and supported with as many direct quotations as possible.[34] At this point, it is usually helpful to share the draft of the report and have a discussion with the rest of the library staff to determine the most actionable results of the focus group and how to present those results as tools for advocacy. After this discussion, recommendations and next steps can be included as the final portion of the report. Ultimately from an advocacy point of view, a plan of action should be determined that identifies the most powerful quotations and conclusions from the group and outlines the best method of communicating them as part of the library's advocacy plan. See chapter 6, "Presenting Data to Get Results," for some ideas.

Virtual Focus Group Options and Considerations

The ideal setting for a focus group is face-to-face. For libraries in rural settings that serve a large geographic area or to reach a district-wide group of adults in a large school system, a virtual focus group may be a viable alternative. Virtual meeting software like the kind used for webinars or applications like Skype, FaceTime, Google Hangout, and other online meeting options may be available. Of course there are some challenges to overcome when taking this approach.

Technology is not always 100 percent reliable. Access to the software and hardware necessary to meet can be the biggest obstacle. It should be obvious that participants must not only be comfortable in the virtual setting but also have access to the chosen format and know how to use it to join a session at a designated time. Frustrations over technology do not promote a positive experience. Moreover, the participants in a virtual group may not be entirely representative, as those without the necessary access, knowledge, or comfort level will be left out. This consideration alone may eliminate the virtual focus group as a possibility. The moderator, too, must be fully versed in the chosen format so that all his or her energy is focused on facilitating the conversation and not on figuring out how to operate the program. Although webcams and devices with built-in cameras can allow for some nonverbal communication cues, the moderator will be more highly dependent upon verbal responses, which may limit the follow-up opportunities more easily identified in person. There will be a greater burden on the moderator to ensure equal participation, and calling on specific people or employing a round-robin format may be even more necessary than in a traditional focus group. That said, the ease with which sessions can be recorded together with opportunities for including audiovisual prompts during the conversation—not to mention the chance to include far-flung participants—are valid reasons to consider virtual focus groups as part of your advocacy arsenal.

Notes

1. "Focus Groups," in *Encyclopedia of Small Business*, 3rd ed. (Detroit: Gale, 2007), Educators Reference Complete.
2. David W. Stewart, Prem N. Shamdasani, and Dennis W. Rook, *Focus Groups: Theory and Practice*, 2nd ed. (Thousand Oaks, CA: SAGE, 2007), 10.
3. James Cox and Keni Brayton Cox, *Your Opinion, Please! How to Build the Best Questionnaires in the Field of Education*, 2nd ed.(Thousand Oaks, CA: Corwin Press, 2008), 71.
4. Kay Bishop and Sandra Hughes-Hassell. "Using Focus Group Interviews to Improve Library Services for Youth," *Teacher Librarian* 32 (October 2004): 10, Educators Reference Complete.

5. William Atkinson, "Keep the Customer Satisfied . . . and Engaged: Ten Tips to Forming a Customer Advisory Council," *EHS Today* 4 (July 2011): pp. F–G, General OneFile.

6. Stewart, Shamdasani, and Rook, *Focus Groups*, 19.

7. Ibid., 19–22.

8. Bishop and Hughes-Hassell, "Using Focus Group Interviews," 8.

9. Stewart, Shamdasani, and Rook, *Focus Groups*, 26.

10. Carter McNamara, "Basics of Conducting Focus Groups," Free Management Library, accessed February 4, 2012, http://managementhelp.org/businessresearch/focus-groups.htm.

11. "Focus Groups."

12. Meghan Cope, "Interviewing," in *Encyclopedia of Human Geography*, ed. Barney Warf (Thousand Oaks, CA: SAGE, 2006), Gale Virtual Reference Library e-book.

13. Karen Becker, "Are You Hearing Voices?," *Quality Progress* 38 (February 2005): 28–35, ProQuest Platinum.

14. McNamara, "Conducting Focus Groups."

15. Becker, "Are You Hearing Voices?"

16. Bishop and Hughes-Hassell, "Using Focus Group Interviews," 9.

17. Stewart, Shamdasani, and Rook, *Focus Groups*, 38.

18. Becker, "Are You Hearing Voices?"

19. Atkinson, "Keep the Customer Satisfied."

20. Stewart, Shamdasani, and Rook, *Focus Groups*, 25.

21. Bishop and Hughes-Hassell, "Using Focus Group Interviews," 11.

22. McNamara, "Conducting Focus Groups."

23. "Focus Groups."

24. Cope, "Interviewing."

25. Bishop and Hughes-Hassell, "Using Focus Group Interviews," 11.

26. Stewart, Shamdasani, and Rook, *Focus Groups*, 23.

27. McNamara, "Conducting Focus Groups."

28. Atkinson, "Keep the Customer Satisfied."

29. Becker, "Are You Hearing Voices?"

30. Ibid.

31. Bishop and Hughes-Hassell, "Using Focus Group Interviews," 11.

32. McNamara, "Conducting Focus Groups."

33. Bishop and Hughes-Hassell, "Using Focus Group Interviews," 11.

34. Ibid.

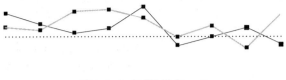

CHAPTER 6

Presenting Data to Get Results

Of all of our inventions for mass communication, pictures still speak the most universally understood language.

—WALT DISNEY

The final and arguably most important step in ensuring that you are heard is to showcase your evidence in an easily understood and compelling way. Today's communications are more visually based than ever, with a smartphone in every pocket, ready to take and receive pictures and loaded with apps to manipulate them. Add Pinterest, Twitter, Facebook, Tumblr, and YouTube, and it seems that everyone is competing to add to the sensory input in our lives. Presenting your data by taking advantage of the visual tools at your disposal is a must. Expertly visualized data is not only professional looking; it is the most appealing and intelligible medium for communicating your evidence. This chapter will focus on guidelines for presenting data in a variety of ways, with an emphasis on creating and framing visual representations of your data for a lasting impression. (For a checklist of things to consider, see appendix C.)

Creating Clarity and Context for Comprehension

Few things are more mind-numbing than an onslaught of numbers. Whether they are hearing them or forced to read them, audiences will quickly lose interest if they have to work to decipher a
crowd of numbers and guess their relevance. Instead, data should
be presented in a clean, simple manner that is easily comprehended.
Context is what makes data compelling. Never express numbers in
isolation. A meaningful context demonstrates a direct connection to
the issue at hand. To use data effectively, you have to clearly understand why this information is worthy of communication. What does
it help you say, and why does it resonate? The bottom line is that
your purpose is not to share the data but to share the ideas behind it.
As Rueben Bronee aptly says, "Numbers aren't messages; they support messages."[1] Creating a table of statistics, calling out figures in a
presentation, or incorporating data in a block of text is a fairly easy
task, but it places the burden of understanding on the audience, and
most people will not invest the time and effort to figure out the significance of the numbers. They'll just tune them (and you) out. Presenting data visually grabs the audience's attention while facilitating
understanding. That data should be expressed in real-world terms
so the audience understands its significance. Tables of numbers, a
multitude of graphs, or lists of percentages are not by themselves
personally meaningful.[2] In many cases a combination of text and
graphics is ideal. Just remember to limit yourself to the main idea
of your message. The One-Question Survey summaries presented
online by Gail K. Dickinson for *Library Media Connection* are great
examples of how to focus on a specific topic and share data visually
while putting it in context with an appropriate amount of text (www
.librarymediaconnection.com/lmc/?page=survey_results).

Penny Johnson, Teen Specialist at the Baraboo Public Library
(Wisconsin), feels strongly that librarians should be proficient in
data visualization techniques. As a "memorable attention grab-
ber," communicating this way makes sense because our brains are

programmed to retain images over words. Johnson believes that two advantages in developing graphic representations are that they are easy to digest (compared, for example, to a multipage report) and that they are likely to be shared through social media and forwarded e-mail messages, a factor that has the potential to exponentially increase the reach and influence of your message.[3]

Techniques for Greater Clarity of Data

Regardless of your method of delivery, the clarity of your data is the most important aspect of your communication plan. Examine your data set and determine if you can parse numbers into more meaningful chunks. For example, to analyze attendance at public library programs, you can break the overall number down in any number of ways. A single number representing an annual attendance figure communicates only how many people participated in a given program in the course of a year. Examining that number through different lenses provides greater clarity. Look at monthly, weekly, daily, or even morning, afternoon, and evening attendance.[4] Categorize by type of program, cost, and who actually participated. How many seniors, parents and children, teens, English-language learners, or adults attended programs? How many and which programs were full with a waiting list, and how many had poor attendance? If your goal is to maintain or increase funding for library programs, then you must depend on these subcategory numbers to communicate a clearer picture of attendance. By breaking down the numbers, you open a multitude of avenues for analysis and may just find the evidence that makes your argument for you.

During the communication stage, ensure that the data you are using speaks directly to your point. For example, so many budget discussions focus on the dollar amount without considering the value of the expenditure. If the library board or principal is balking over a dollar figure, fight back with your own numbers. Don't respond that the cost will cover one additional database, but that patrons or the school community will gain access to 3,000 new journals—an average of 30,000 new articles a month—that were not available to them before.[5] Keep the conversation on the benefits and the return on investment. In a school setting, focus on the impact on students. Tying an expenditure to demonstrated needs from a survey or focus group would strengthen the argument even more.

Clarity of data should transfer to any visual that you create. Nothing should distract from your content. So although there are many apps, web-based programs, and presentation software tools that claim to give an edge in presenting data, show restraint. A flurry of colors, 3-D effects, or animations risk driving attention away from your point.[6] Familiar and widely used software programs such as Apple's Pages or Microsoft Publisher for design, Excel for spreadsheets and charts, or PowerPoint for slides can be a great starting point in developing your own visuals. For creating tables, Excel and Microsoft Word are equally capable; be sure to avoid a lot of rules or shading, which can detract from your message (see fig. 6.1). The more basic but free options from Google can also be useful. Always be straightforward about the source of your data when incorporating it into your written, spoken, or visual presentations. Trust your audience to judge the validity of your claim with full disclosure, and give credit to other sources.[7] Not doing so weakens and often nullifies the effectiveness of the data.

Gareth Public Library 2013 Print Circulation

	Jan	Feb	Mar	Apr	May	Jun	Jul	Aug	Sep	Oct	Nov	Dec
Adult	2399	2172	2158	1967	2282	2292	2156	2135	1710	1815	1651	1317
YA	351	221	279	302	363	418	396	312	244	253	270	298
Children	1991	2059	1924	1697	1936	3263	2451	1673	1646	1814	1772	1844
Total	4741	4452	4361	3966	4581	5973	5003	4120	3600	3882	3693	3459

Figure 6.1. Tables are good at presenting a lot of data in an organized way. Avoid excess rules and shading, which can detract from the message. This table highlights the months with the least circulation in each category.

Context Is Everything

As you frame your data, you are choosing the context in which to present it. How you introduce it and explain its significance will make the difference between powerful and not-so-powerful communication. Emphasize the human side to your figures. If you want to emphasize the popularity of a certain children's program at your library, for example, a photograph of patrons standing along the perimeter of the room with children crowded on the floor, mesmerized by what they are seeing and hearing, will speak quite effectively to your point.[8] Each data point represents something potentially significant in the real world, and your job as an advocate is to make that story come alive. Without that human connection, data is meaningless to your purpose.[9]

Looking at relationships among your data and between data sets is the most effective way to draw context. Humans need to link new information to prior knowledge in order to comprehend and remember it long term. One technique is to compare and contrast your data with other recognizable references. Say you are facing a tough battle over a library closure. You've been given the task of demonstrating the relevancy of libraries to people's lives. Opening your presentation by stating that there are more than 16,000 public libraries in the United States may sound impressive, but it will not necessarily resonate with your audience and is likely to be forgotten. On the other hand, a graphic that illustrates that, as of December 2011, the total number of public library branches in the United States was 2,600 more than the total number of McDonald's franchises is almost guaranteed to have an impact. People will understand the comparison and perhaps be surprised, while also being more likely to remember your point—that libraries are a part of many communities and, as such, affect citizens' daily lives.

How you choose to express a fact is up to you, but you want to aim for the greatest impact. A $1,500 cut to a school library technology budget may not sound so bad to the average person. Putting that number in context changes the impact if, for example, the entire technology budget is $3,000. To make your case even stronger, do the math and express the figure as a percentage—a 50 percent reduction in the ability to purchase technology is an even better expression of the severity of the cut. Finally, consider the need to place a number in context over time to illustrate a trend.[10] If there have been consecutive years of technology cuts, include that information. Place it even further in context by, for example, showing the increase in the past few years of students without access to technology in their homes. Express this number in a relatable context as well: "Three out of every ten of our students do not have Internet access at home." Statistics about e-book use, Facebook activity, budget cuts, and the number of classes receiving instruction from librarians all take on different shades of meaning when measured against the past.

Charts and Graphs

Typical graphics produced from a spreadsheet might be considered dry and boring, but as a simple tool to illustrate a data set, they are the easiest to produce and understand. Graphics of any kind should act as a summary of your data that can be easily understood by others.[11] Bar and line graphs along with pie charts are the most common visual representations of statistics, but there are significant considerations for using them effectively. Try to avoid overwhelming the audience with data.[12] There is a temptation to put it all out there after spending so much time planning, collecting, and analyzing. You can always provide more statistics if asked, but you will lose your audience's attention if what you have presented is too much to digest. Match the type of graphic with the data at hand. A bar graph is best used to compare different data points that can be ranked by size or importance (see fig. 6.2). A line graph, which

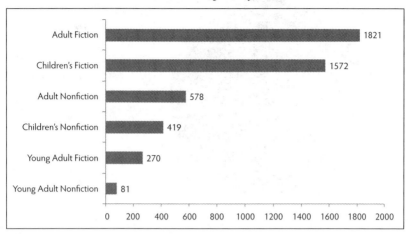

Figure 6.2. Bar graphs can be used to rank data by size or importance.

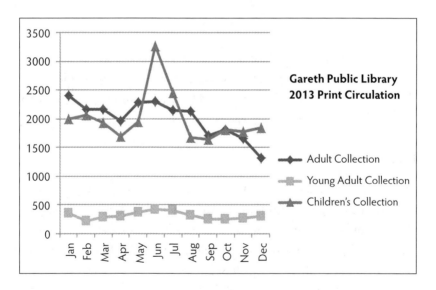

Figure 6.3. Line graphs illustrate trends over time.

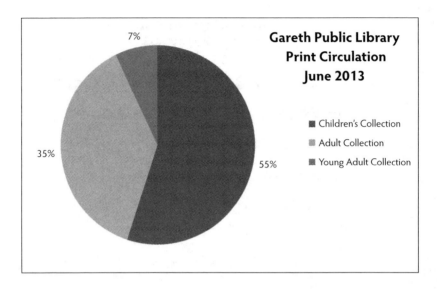

Figure 6.4. Pie charts, which show the relationships of parts to a whole, must add up to 100 percent (after accounting for rounding of individual values).

shows the position of data points relative to each other as they fluctuate over time, is good at showing trends (fig. 6.3). A pie chart illustrates the relationship of parts to a whole and must represent the entire data set, or 100 percent (fig. 6.4).[13]

Design Tips

Once the data set has been identified, create your graph or chart by following a simple progression of steps. The first step is to research the elements of your chart, including any permissions and source citations that may be necessary. Next, edit your data by filtering through it carefully to simplify what you want to express without unfairly manipulating the results. Then, after you have chosen the most appropriate format, carefully plot your numbers to create the chart or graph. Be sure to use a simple font, appealing color choices, and clear labels. Finally, review your graphic to ensure that it communicates what you intend it to, remembering to double-check your figures and, if you can, get another person's read on it to test comprehension.[14] No matter the type of chart or graph, provide all the information needed for understanding it on the graphic itself.[15] A key or legend might make your graphic a little more difficult to understand at first glance, but certainly make use of one if necessary. Use color sparingly, and any colors that you do use should help convey meaning. Provide contrast through different shades of the same color family or by using bold type or lines for emphasis. This approach is also effective when graphics have to be reproduced in grayscale. Especially for readability, size and white space are also important considerations. Labels should be large enough to see clearly, and bars or data points on bar and line graphs should be a proportionate distance from each other.

Some experts in data visualization recommend staying away from pie charts because of their inherent limitations. If more than one of the segments is no more than a small sliver of the pie, the chart will look crowded and become difficult to label; the same is true if there are too many segments. Color choice or shading is extremely important—there should be significant contrast or a single color with clear boarders to prevent segments from merging together. Highlight the most significant segment by assigning it a darker shade. For balance, the largest segment of the pie should start at the top at noon and open up clockwise to the right.[16] For an excellent, hands-on tutorial of best practices, take the online "Graph Design I.Q. Test" at Perceptual Edge (http://www.perceptualedge .com/files/GraphDesignIQ.html).

Focus on Accuracy

Perhaps the people who look at statistics skeptically have been misled by manipulated data. Sometimes the data is perfectly valid, but the expression of it is deceiving. Most measurements can be presented either as a percentage or as a raw number. And, whereas the communicator naturally wants to present information in the most advantageous form, there are circumstances in which good ethical practice makes the choice clear. As noted in chapter 3, "Working with the Power of Statistics," percentages and averages are best avoided with small data sets. For example, percentages calculated from just a few numbers and plotted on a line graph might show a steep slope that misrepresents the bigger picture. It is also important to use original numbers without rounding when making calculations and analyzing results. Some rounding may be necessary for the purposes of presenting the data to your audience, but it should wait until that point to maintain the integrity of the results.[17]

Verify that the design of your chart or graph communicates a true and representative picture of your data. Naomi Robbins, in her blog *Effective Graphs*, explains, for example, how changing the aspect ratio on a line graph can drastically alter the appearance of a trend, making it seem more or less severe without changing numbers or plot points (see fig. 6.5). Not starting at zero in a bar or line graph can also exaggerate a trend (fig. 6.6). Unfortunately, many readers don't take the time to examine labels to get a better understanding of what they are seeing and are left with a decidedly false impression.[18] Reviewing the final product for accuracy is also a must. Any small typo, misplotted data point, or confusing label can lead readers to a different conclusion than the one intended. Be sure to explain the meaning of any symbols or colors, and pay particular attention to the labels on the axes in line graphs. Don't assume that the meaning behind your graphic is self-evident. Whatever form your graphic takes, it should be expressed as simply as possible and function as a visual summary of what you want to communicate.[19] The most effective charts and graphs will expose the more salient patterns or relationships that you have discovered through your analysis of the data and, in turn, answer some important questions. For example, what has consistently stayed the same? What has changed, and when and how? What has been the overall trend over time? What are the most significant parts that make up the whole? How do the different measurements, factors, and elements relate to each other?

Gareth Public Library
Young Adult Print Circulation, 2013

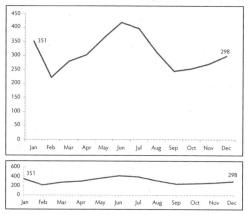
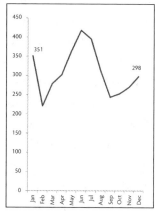
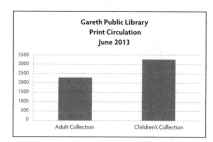

Figure 6.5. These three line graphs all show the same data, but the one on the right and at the bottom exaggerate the trend by skewing the aspect ratio of the figure.

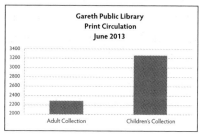

Figure 6.6. Avoid bar graphs like the one on the right. The one on the left, by starting at zero, gives a more accurate picture of the data.

Infographics: Telling a Story through Data and Design

As an advocate, you are constantly seeking the gift of attention. Well-conceived infographics are especially effective at gaining attention because of their novelty factor. People take note of what appears to be visually unique in their environment. Therefore, communicating in a unique visual way has the potential to arrest your audience's attention.[20] Infographics have become an increasingly

popular method to visually communicate data. Always a staple for
news graphics, software and do-it-yourself ingenuity have made
them accessible to everyone. What separates an infographic from
a chart, graph, or list of statistics is the visual organization and
appeal. Usually colorful and utilizing a creative layout of pictures
and fonts, infographics are stand-alone pieces that contain all the
details necessary to understand a given statistical narrative. Data
visualization expert David McCandless refers to the concept of the
information map. This map requires the viewer to blend the languages of eye and mind together to create new understanding.[21]
Randy Krum, author of the blog *Cool Infographics*, explains that
infographics have to be carefully considered. They must be informative while also attracting attention. They can't be boring, but at
the same time they can't be overly complex.[22] The bottom line is
that for an infographic to be successful, it must adhere to certain
design principles and communicate meaningful information while
being truly unique—to the point that it gets noticed.

Three common elements of successful infographics are rich
content, inviting visuals, and sophisticated execution.[23] *Communication Nation* blogger Dave Gray has written an extensive definition of the term *infographic*, but the most distinctive characteristic
is that it should reveal information that is otherwise lost in a crowd
of data.[24] For an infographic to be successful, there should be a
moment of revelation as the viewer recognizes something new and
significant. Therefore, infographics may not be an appropriate form
of communication unless the message told by the data is truly significant or surprising. As with all tools of successful advocacy, the
most critical consideration in producing an infographic is the strategic forethought that takes place beforehand. If you jump immediately into the design, your message is likely to be off target. The
same cautions about working with statistics apply to creating infographics. An appealing design is worthless if the information that it
depends on isn't statistically sound.[25] Just as important is whether
the infographic does what you intend it to do. Does it successfully

communicate the significant message you had in mind, the one that will resonate with your audience by communicating to them the information they need?

If a graphics department or specialized software is not on hand to create an infographic, there are other ways to produce an effective one. The infographic shown in figure 6.7 is a simplistic design that generated multiple conversations, and I produced it in less than an hour using PowerPoint and some stock photography. I started by thinking about what I wanted to communicate to my administration and staff about the library during National Library Week. Occasionally, a teacher or administrator would stop in to the library for a brief moment and comment about how nice and quiet it was. I always had the urge to point to the jam-packed schedule listed on the whiteboard and call them back in ten minutes when our four scheduled classes had decided to arrive at the same time and say, "Not so nice and quiet now, is it?" I needed a way to convey how well used the library is to those who aren't there all the time. That led to the thought that while I can show our class sign-ups and keep track of the teaching we were doing, a major indicator of the library's value to the school was not being communicated. Our high school students could choose to visit the library on their own, before school, after school, during lunch, during a study hall period, and of course with a pass from a teacher during class. The previous year we had instituted an electronic sign-in for student visitors—they simply entered their student ID numbers on a number pad attached to a laptop. This populated a Microsoft Access database that was connected to our student information system. The student's name and the time were automatically shown on the screen upon signing in, and we gathered records of all visitors. The nature of the database allowed us to run queries showing total number of visitors, gender and ethnicity, repeat visitors, time of day most visitors arrived, and so on. I had a tremendous amount of data at my fingertips, and now I had an information need and an intended audience. I wanted to counter some false impressions with the true picture of the library's place in meeting student needs. I could have listed these same numbers in a chart or table, but that wouldn't grab anyone's attention. So I decided to highlight the numbers in an easy-to-understand and appealing way by creating my first infographic.

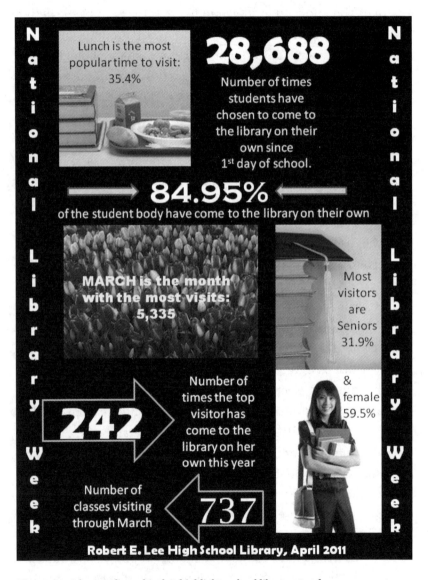

Figure 6.7. A basic infographic that highlights school library attendance.

I had plenty of data, but had to identify just those data points that would speak to my message that the library is a place that students freely choose to visit on a regular basis. I placed what I thought was the most attention-getting number (28,688 visits from September through March) on the upper-right corner with the boldest and brightest font. I followed with the second most important figure (84.5 percent of the student body had visited the library on their own) in the center with the two arrows pointing to it. I then carefully placed the other figures to maintain balance and included representative stock photographs. I had my wow factor of the student with the most individual visits (242, about two per school day) in large type balancing the lower half of the design. I created a black background on the PowerPoint slide with bright colors and white text for contrast. I made sure the arrangement appeared symmetrical and clean, then saved the slide as a picture. I sent it embedded in a staff e-mail with a paragraph highlighting the classes and lessons we were teaching that week. My purpose was to demonstrate our value to the school by showcasing a week's teaching in a short narrative balanced by evidence in the infographic that when given a choice, students wanted to be in the library. Based on the comments I received from that single e-mail, teachers and staff received the message that the Lee High School Library is a valuable asset to the school's instructional program and a busy, welcoming place students choose to visit. While successful, there are some changes that may have made it even more effective. The infographic is functional, but not sophisticated. With different software, it could have looked more professional. And I feel that I missed an opportunity to have followed up with more powerful information. The infographic failed to answer the question "Why?" A third of all visitors were seniors. Was the library meeting their needs better than younger students? Did the fact that they had been in the school the longest give them more time to see the value of using the library? Or was there some other practical reason that more seniors chose to be in the library on their own? With 84.95 percent of the student body

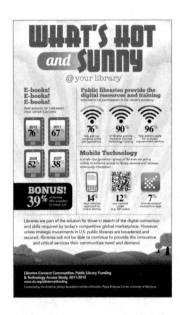

Figure 6.8. A conceptual info-graphic (broken here into two parts to fit the printed page).

SOURCE: AMERICAN LIBRARY ASSOCIATION, OFFICE FOR RESEARCH AND STATISTICS.

Figure 6.9. A section of the infographic from figure 6.8.

SOURCE: AMERICAN LIBRARY ASSOCIATION, OFFICE FOR RESEARCH AND STATISTICS.

visiting at least once, what was the story behind those who never visited? Finally, an interview with the top ten visitors to the library in a focus group to find out why they came so frequently would have provided a great opportunity to gather more information to share in our advocacy efforts.

Professional graphic designers are able to create more sophisticated infographics. See the example here from the American Library Association's Office for Research and Statistics (figure 6.8). The weather theme ties a tremendous amount of information together from an important study and organizes it effectively into challenges and areas of success. The numbers are distinct, with clear text putting them in context and sources credited as necessary. Examined as a whole, this infographic reflects the complete story of the competing forces of budget shortfalls and increased need for services facing public libraries at the time. Figure 6.9 highlights a segment of the infographic that focuses on the disparity between demand for services and falling budgets. Each segment was thought out completely so that any one part of the overall whole could be used individually in a variety of messages. Appealing, clear, meaningful and effective, this is a prime example of a successful conceptual infographic.

PowerPoint Design

There are many presentation software and Web 2.0 tools that offer alternatives to Microsoft PowerPoint, but none are as widely used. Audiences complain of experiencing "death by PowerPoint," but when used effectively, PowerPoint is a powerful tool for delivering visually enhanced information to a large group or through a webinar or virtual meeting scenario. The key is in the design. Develop slides that complement your presentation but are not the sole focus. The audience needs to connect with you personally as a speaker and advocate. One strategy for ensuring that viewers don't focus solely on the slides is to limit the text and have a simple graphic or

image that either summarizes your point or represents it. Long pas-
sages read straight from a slide are rarely engaging, but that doesn't
mean you shouldn't spend time explaining data that appears on the
screen if necessary. Certainly, putting up complex tables or long lists
of numbers is not effective, but don't be afraid to briefly walk the
audience through a graph or infographic to make sure its message
is clear. Keep the slides as clean and uncluttered as possible, and
avoid complicated or irrelevant backgrounds, which simply distract
and make it more difficult to decipher the content.[26] Pay close attention to your use of color. A bright red graphic on a dark blue background may look fine on your computer screen, but how will it look
when displayed through the projector? It's best to put light-colored
objects or text on a darker background and vice versa. Text size is
critical. Presenters apologize all the time for having to read slides
to an audience because the text or labeling is too small, but if they
knew it would be a problem, they should have made the effort to
avoid creating such a slide. The same information could have been
provided in a handout. Use of any clip art that is not essential for
communicating your message is likely to appear amateurish. Photographs, even generic stock photos, are immensely more appealing—
although the rule of relevance still applies.[27] Finally, PowerPoint's
SmartArt function provides an effortless way to create professional-
looking touches that organize your presentation.

Leaving a Lasting Impression

Consider what your audience will take away from your communication efforts. What you present as a rationale or evidence for your
point of view will have to stand on its own merits once you are no
longer there to clarify and defend it. Data visualization is such an
effective communication technique not only because it makes your
evidence accessible but also because it makes it portable. Putting an
infographic or chart on a website, posting it on Facebook or Twitter,

even providing it in a handout makes it conveniently available for sharing with others. That's a huge advantage to spreading your message, but it is also a potential liability. Once your product has been posted, it can be difficult to rein it back in. A poorly conceived or executed idea will live out in the world to be judged or misunderstood. So review your products with a critical eye and get feedback from others. Only then will you be ready to step forward with confidence and exert your influence.

Notes

1. Rueben Bronee, "Writing That Counts: Three Ways to Use Numbers Creatively to Communicate," *ContentWise*, January 2009, www.becontentwise.com/Article.php?art_num=5109.
2. Lila Herndon Vizzard, e-mail message to author, October 22, 2012.
3. Penny Johnson, e-mail message to author, October 8, 2012.
4. Ibid.
5. Karen J. Wanamaker, "Flaunt It If You've Got It!," in *Marketing Your Library: Tips and Tools That Work*, ed. Carol Smallwood, Vera Gubnitskaia, and Kerol Harrod (Jefferson, NC: McFarland, 2012), 107–8.
6. Dona M. Wong, *The Wall Street Journal Guide to Information Graphics: The Dos and Don'ts of Presenting Data, Facts, and Figures* (New York: W. W. Norton, 2010), 13.
7. Nathan Yau, *Visualize This: The FlowingData Guide to Design, Visualization, and Statistics* (Indianapolis: Wiley, 2011), 19.
8. Robin Williams, *The Non-Designer's Presentation Book* (Berkeley, CA: Peachpit Press, 2010), 68.
9. Yau, *Visualize This*, 2.
10. Wong, *Wall Street Journal Guide*, 24.
11. Mark Anawis, "Carefully Orchestrated Duet Aids Decisions: Achieving the Right Balance between Graphics and Statistical Analysis," *Scientific Computing* 28 (January–February 2011): 27–29, General OneFile.
12. Sandra Nelson, "Presenting Data," in *The PLA Reader for Public Library Directors and Managers*, ed. Kathleen M. Hughes (New York: Neal-Schuman, 2009), 206.

13. Ibid., 215.

14. Wong, *Wall Street Journal Guide*, 20.

15. Ibid., 45.

16. Ibid., 65–77.

17. Ibid., 25–27.

18. Naomi Robbins, "How to Exaggerate Trends in Graphs," *Effective Graphs* (blog), September 12, 2012, http://blogs.forbes.com/naomirobbins/2012/09/12/misleading-by-changing-the-aspect-ratio-to-hide-variation-or-exaggerate-trends-in-graphs/.

19. Yau, *Visualize This*, 8.

20. Mark Smiciklas, *The Power of Infographics: Using Pictures to Communicate and Connect with Your Audiences* (Indianapolis: Que, 2012), Kindle e-book, chap. 1.

21. David McCandless, "David McCandless: The Beauty of Data Visualization," Ted (video), 2010. www.ted.com/talks/lang/en/david_mccandless_the_beauty_of_data_visualization.html.

22. Randy Krum, "10 Tips for Designing Infographics," *Digital News Gathering*, April 24, 2010, http://digitalnewsgathering.wordpress.com/2010/04/24/10-tips-for-designing-infographics/.

23. Wong, *Wall Street Journal Guide*, 14.

24. Dave Gray, "What Is an Infographic?," *Communication Nation* (blog), November 11, 2007, http://communicationnation.blogspot.com/2007/04/what-is-infographic.html.

25. Smiciklas, *Power of Infographics*, chap. 2.

26. Williams, *Non-Designer's Presentation Book*, 46.

27. Ibid., 54.

Appendix A

Survey Checklist

Communication objective:

_____

_____

The planning process has included

- ❑ An examination of different survey formats to determine the most appropriate one
- ❑ Input from the library staff
- ❑ A timeline and budget
- ❑ A delivery method for getting the survey to participants
- ❑ A review of previous surveys to determine the need for trend data
- ❑ The determination of a sample size or census
- ❑ Accommodations for non-English-speaking participants
- ❑ A plan for nonrespondents
- ❑ Guidelines for analyzing results and creating a summary report

Survey questions

- ❑ Directly relate to the communication objective
- ❑ Are clear, concise, and unbiased
- ❑ Follow rules of validity
- ❑ Are placed in a strategic order
- ❑ Have been vetted by a pilot group
- ❑ Are accompanied by an introduction

Survey participants

- ❑ Are representative of the community
- ❑ Include both library users and nonusers as appropriate
- ❑ Number above the recommended sample size or, for a census, include all members
- ❑ Have access to raw results and/or summary report

Appendix B

Focus Group Checklist

Communication objective:

_____

_____

The planning process has included

- ❑ A timeline for preparation
- ❑ Input from the library staff
- ❑ A review of recent surveys for results that need further exploration
- ❑ Provisions for food, drink, and/or other incentives
- ❑ Identification of a moderator and an observer
- ❑ A plan for recording the session
- ❑ Guidelines for analyzing results and creating a summary report

Focus group questions

- ❑ Directly relate to the communication objective
- ❑ Are concise
- ❑ Have been read aloud to check for clarity

❑ Begin with a general focus and then become more specific

❑ Conclude with a brief evaluation sheet for participants

Focus group participants

❑ Are representative of the community

❑ Include both library users and nonusers

❑ Are within the optimum number range of six to ten individuals

❑ Have a comfortable setting with

    ❑ Minimal distractions

    ❑ Proper lighting, temperature, space

❑ Are meeting at a time and location that is convenient for them

Appendix C

Data Presentation Checklist

Communication objective:

_____

_____

The presentation of data

- ❏ Is directly related to the communication objective
- ❏ Explores relationships among statistics
    - ❏ By examining subgroups or categories
    - ❏ By looking at trends over time
- ❏ Reflects the needs, interests, and background of the intended audience
- ❏ Is interesting

The graphic

- ❏ Can stand alone
- ❏ Is simply and clearly presented
- ❏ Includes a sufficient balance between image and text
- ❏ Conveys one main idea
- ❏ Enhances understanding of content

❑ Includes credit/citation for information or images borrowed from other sources

❑ Is in the best medium/format for conveying the message

❑ Looks professional, and

    ❑ Uses color to enhance meaning

    ❑ Contains text of a readable size

    ❑ Is properly labeled for clarity and comprehension

The data

❑ Directly supports the communication objective

❑ Has been verified for accuracy

❑ Is broken down into meaningful chunks

❑ Is cited to the relevant source(s)

❑ Has been pared down to be relevant and significant

Appendix D

Birmingham Public Library Patron Survey

Patron suggestions are the most important resource we have in determining what materials and services to offer at Birmingham Public Library. This survey will give you the opportunity to make valuable and specific suggestions to us. Please take a moment and provide us with this important information.

1. How often do you use the Birmingham Public Library (BPL)?
   - ❏ More than once a month
   - ❏ About once a month
   - ❏ Once every six months
   - ❏ 2–3 times per year
   - ❏ This is my first visit

2. Do you have a current BPL library card?
   - ❏ Yes
   - ❏ No

3. Check all BPL materials/services you have used in the past year:
   - ❏ Internet access on library computers
   - ❏ Wi-Fi access for personal computers
   - ❏ DVDs
   - ❏ CDs (music)
   - ❏ Audio books on CD
   - ❏ Downloadable audio books

- ❑ Large-print books
- ❑ Children's story hour
- ❑ Children's summer reading program
- ❑ BPL web page
- ❑ Magazines
- ❑ Holds/reserves
- ❑ Other

4. Check adult programs of interest to you
   - ❑ Informational/educational
   - ❑ Author readings & discussions
   - ❑ Entertainment
   - ❑ Arts & crafts
   - ❑ Book groups
   - ❑ Gaming
   - ❑ Not interested in attending programs

5. Check all reasons for using the Birmingham Public Library
   - ❑ Borrow best-sellers
   - ❑ Borrow other fiction books
   - ❑ Borrow nonfiction books
   - ❑ Perform research for personal use
   - ❑ Perform research for school projects
   - ❑ Borrow DVDs
   - ❑ Borrow CDs
   - ❑ Borrow audio books
   - ❑ Use copy machine
   - ❑ Read magazines/newspapers
   - ❑ Use Wi-Fi access for personal computer
   - ❑ Use the Internet on library computers
   - ❑ Use government publications
   - ❑ Obtain income tax forms
   - ❑ Use children's collection
   - ❑ Attend story-hour or children's programs
   - ❑ Use the teen collection

❑ Obtain information for home/car repairs

❑ Study/work

❑ Attend a meeting

❑ Use reference materials in library

❑ Browse collection

❑ Faxing

❑ Other

6. Have your visits to the library been successful?

❑ Yes

❑ No

❑ Sometimes

7. Check all the reasons for unsuccessful visits to the library

❑ Item was checked out

❑ Library had no material on the subject

❑ I could not find the material

❑ Staff could not find the material

❑ Computers were not working

❑ Wi-Fi was not working

❑ All computers were in use

❑ I don't know how to use the computers

❑ Staff had to request material from another library

❑ Other

8. Check children's programs important to you

❑ Summer reading programs

❑ Informational or educational

❑ Entertainment

❑ Story-hour

❑ Not interested in children's programming

9. Check all areas that you think need more material:

❑ General nonfiction

❑ General fiction

❑ Mystery

- ❏ Science fiction
- ❏ Romance
- ❏ Western
- ❏ Religion/philosophy
- ❏ History
- ❏ Arts/culture
- ❏ Science/technology
- ❏ Health/medicine
- ❏ Travel
- ❏ Self-help
- ❏ Biography
- ❏ Large-print books
- ❏ Magazines/newspapers
- ❏ Children's materials
- ❏ Other

10. Check preferred formats of library materials
- ❏ Books
- ❏ CDs
- ❏ DVDs
- ❏ Downloadable audio books
- ❏ Online databases
- ❏ Other

11. Check all that would improve BPL technology
- ❏ More computers for Internet access
- ❏ More computers to access library collection
- ❏ Improved Wi-Fi accessibility
- ❏ More online databases
- ❏ Other

12. Check all describing the service you received at the library
- ❏ Staff was helpful and pleasant
- ❏ Staff was too busy to help me
- ❏ I did not ask for help

❏ Staff did not have knowledge to help me
❏ Other

13. Check all that describe the library's atmosphere
    ❏ Friendly
    ❏ Noisy
    ❏ Safe
    ❏ Comfortable
    ❏ Fun
    ❏ Orderly
    ❏ Helpful staff
    ❏ Quiet
    ❏ Boring
    ❏ Exciting
    ❏ Clean
    ❏ Other

14. How do you find out about Birmingham Public Library
    services and events?
    ❏ BPL website calendar
    ❏ Birmingham News
    ❏ Radio advertisements
    ❏ Television
    ❏ Word-of-mouth
    ❏ Internet search
    ❏ Other

15. Your educational level
    ❏ Little or no high school
    ❏ High school graduate
    ❏ Vocational/technical school
    ❏ Some college
    ❏ College graduate
    ❏ Graduate degree

16. Your Age Group
- ❏ 18–29
- ❏ 30–39
- ❏ 40–49
- ❏ 50–59
- ❏ 60 or older

17. Your gender
- ❏ Female
- ❏ Male

18. Your zip code: _____

USED WITH PERMISSION FROM THE BIRMINGHAM PUBLIC LIBRARY (ALABAMA).
WWW.SURVEYMONKEY.COM/S.ASPX?SM=GDOY7YKRYACWHTW1Z3WTEA_3D_3D.

Appendix E

Sample Student Survey,
Robert E. Lee High School

Library Experience

1. The library staff is welcoming to me.
    ❑ Never   ❑ Sometimes
    ❑ Often   ❑ Always   ❑ Don't know

    Optional comment: _____

2. When I have questions while in the library, a staff member can answer them.
    ❑ Never   ❑ Sometimes
    ❑ Often   ❑ Always   ❑ Don't know

    Optional comment: _____

3. The library meets my needs for school assignments.
    ❑ Never   ❑ Sometimes
    ❑ Often   ❑ Always   ❑ Don't know

    Optional comment: _____

4. I like being in the library.
    ❑ Never   ❑ Sometimes
    ❑ Often   ❑ Always   ❑ Don't know

    Optional comment: _____

Facility and Resources

1. There's a library computer available for me when I need one.
   ❑ Never ❑ Sometimes
   ❑ Often ❑ Always ❑ Don't know

   Optional comment: _____

2. The library is a comfortable place.
   ❑ Never ❑ Sometimes
   ❑ Often ❑ Always ❑ Don't know

   Optional comment: _____

3. I check out books for personal reading from the library.
   ❑ Never ❑ Sometimes
   ❑ Often ❑ Always ❑ Don't know

   Optional comment: _____

4. I check out books related to research or my class assignments from the library.
   ❑ Never ❑ Sometimes
   ❑ Often ❑ Always ❑ Don't know

   Optional comment: _____

5. I use books in the library for my research or class assignments that I don't need to check out.
   ❑ Never ❑ Sometimes
   ❑ Often ❑ Always ❑ Don't know

   Optional comment: _____

6. I use online databases at school.
   ❑ Never   ❑ Sometimes
   ❑ Often   ❑ Always   ❑ Don't know

   Optional comment: _____

7. I use online databases from home.
   ❑ Never   ❑ Sometimes
   ❑ Often   ❑ Always   ❑ Don't know

   Optional comment: _____

8. I have used the following databases either at school or at
   home (select all that you have ever used before):
   ❑ ABC-Clio
   ❑ Biography Resource Center
   ❑ CQ Researcher
   ❑ Gale Virtual Reference Library
   ❑ Grolier Online
   ❑ JSTOR
   ❑ Opposing Viewpoints
   ❑ ProQuest
   ❑ Science Resource Center
   ❑ SIRS
   ❑ Soundzabound
   ❑ Student Resource Center
   ❑ World Book Online

   Optional comment: _____

Teaching

1. The librarians are prepared to work with my class when we arrive.
   ❑ Never   ❑ Sometimes
   ❑ Often   ❑ Always   ❑ Don't know

   Optional comment: _____

2. The lessons the librarians provide are helpful.
   ❑ Never   ❑ Sometimes
   ❑ Often   ❑ Always   ❑ Don't know

   Optional comment: _____

3. The librarians can help me with technology.
   ❑ Never   ❑ Sometimes
   ❑ Often   ❑ Always   ❑ Don't know

   Optional comment: _____

4. The librarians recommend helpful resources for my assignments.
   ❑ Never   ❑ Sometimes
   ❑ Often   ❑ Always   ❑ Don't know

   Optional comment: _____

5. The librarians are helpful when I need to cite my sources.
   ❑ Never   ❑ Sometimes
   ❑ Often   ❑ Always   ❑ Don't know

   Optional comment: _____

6. The librarians recommend books for me to read.
   ❑ Never   ❑ Sometimes
   ❑ Often   ❑ Always   ❑ Don't know

   Optional comment: _____

Usage

1. I come to the library before school.
    ❑ Never ❑ Sometimes
    ❑ Often ❑ Always ❑ Don't know

    Optional comment: _____

2. I come to the library after school.
    ❑ Never ❑ Sometimes
    ❑ Often ❑ Always ❑ Don't know

    Optional comment: _____

3. I come to the library during lunch.
    ❑ Never ❑ Sometimes
    ❑ Often ❑ Always ❑ Don't know

    Optional comment: _____

4. I get a pass from a teacher to come to the library during class.
    ❑ Never ❑ Sometimes
    ❑ Often ❑ Always ❑ Don't know

    Optional comment: _____

5. This year, the number of times I've come to the library WITH ANY CLASS is:
    ❑ 0 ❑ 1–5 ❑ 6–10 ❑ More than 10 times

    Optional comment: _____

6. This year, the number of times I've come to the library ON MY OWN is:
    ❑ 0 ❑ 1–5 ❑ 6–10 ❑ More than 10 times

    Optional comment: _____

Comments

1. The best thing about the library is: _____

_____

2. If I could change one thing about the library it would be:

_____

3. Additional comments (optional)? _____

_____

Appendix F

Sample Teacher Survey, Robert E. Lee High School

Library Usage

1. I teach (select all that apply):
   - ❑ English
   - ❑ Social Studies
   - ❑ Math
   - ❑ Special Education
   - ❑ Advanced Academic courses
   - ❑ ESOL
   - ❑ PE/Health
   - ❑ Performing Arts
   - ❑ Visual Arts
   - ❑ Business
   - ❑ World Languages
   - ❑ Career and Technical Education
   - ❑ I am a school specialist
   - ❑ Other

2. I have used the following databases either at school or from home (select all that apply):
   - ❑ ABC-Clio
   - ❑ Biography Resource Center
   - ❑ CQ Researcher
   - ❑ Gale Virtual Reference Library
   - ❑ JSTOR

❑ Opposing Viewpoints

❑ ProQuest

❑ Science Resource Center

❑ Literature Resource Center

❑ SIRS

❑ World Book Online

❑ Grolier Online

❑ Academic OneFile

❑ Education Research Complete

❑ Health and Wellness Resource Center

❑ Business and Company Resource Center

3. This year I've used the library to (select all that apply):

❑ Check out a book

❑ Check out a video/DVD

❑ Check out equipment

❑ Get help with technology

❑ Troubleshoot equipment problems

❑ Get help with personal research related to my teaching or a course I am taking

❑ Locate resources

❑ Other (please specify): _____

Library Instruction

1. This year I have brought my classes to the library for any reason:

❑ 0   ❑ 1–3   ❑ More than 3 times

Optional comment: _____

2. This year I have collaborated with the librarians to develop a lesson or activity either in the library or in the classroom.

❑ Yes ❑ No

Optional comment: _____

3. This year I have brought my classes to the library to (select all that apply):

❑ Research

❑ Receive a lesson from the librarians

❑ Check out books

❑ Use the computers or other technology

❑ n/a

Optional comment: _____

4. The librarians are prepared to work with my classes when we arrive.

❑ Never ❑ Sometimes

❑ Often ❑ Always ❑ n/a

Optional comment: _____

5. The lessons the librarians provide are helpful.

❑ Never ❑ Sometimes

❑ Often ❑ Always ❑ Don't know

Optional comment: _____

6. The librarians are helpful working with students individually.

❑ Never ❑ Sometimes

❑ Often ❑ Always ❑ Don't know

Optional comment: _____

7. The librarians help my students with technology.
   ❑ Never   ❑ Sometimes
   ❑ Often   ❑ Always   ❑ Don't know

   Optional comment: _____

8. The librarians recommend helpful resources for my assignments.
   ❑ Never   ❑ Sometimes
   ❑ Often   ❑ Always   ❑ n/a

   Optional comment: _____

Comments

1. The best thing about the library is: _____

   _____

2. If I could change one thing about the library it would be (you may add your name to your comment if you'd like a response): _____

   _____

3. Additional comments (optional)? _____

   _____

Appendix G

Westborough Public School Library Survey (Faculty)

Faculty Satisfaction Survey

The Librarians of the Westborough Public Schools are conducting this survey as part of our process of creating a Long Range Plan for our library program. It is our goal to meet your needs and to improve library services.

Thank you for taking time to participate. Your input is appreciated!

1. School I represent:
   ❑ Armstrong ❑ Fales ❑ Hastings
   ❑ Mill Pond ❑ Gibbons ❑ High School

2. The library resources I use most with classes are (select all that apply):
   ❑ Fiction books
   ❑ Nonfiction books
   ❑ Reference books
   ❑ Audio books
   ❑ Internet
   ❑ eBooks
   ❑ DVD titles
   ❑ Databases
   ❑ Newspapers

❑ Magazines

❑ Wireless reading devices

❑ Other (please specify): _____

3. Library services that I use (select all that apply):

❑ Research skills lessons (techniques for searching and evaluating information)

❑ Using databases—website credibility

❑ Works cited

❑ Resources for research units/class work

❑ Collaboration on research lessons/units

❑ Reader's advisory

❑ Other (please specify): _____

4. I use materials from the library for (select all that apply):

❑ Reading for pleasure

❑ Finding books for students

❑ Research skills lessons (techniques for searching and evaluation information)

❑ Using databases—website credibility

❑ Works cited

❑ Collaboration on research units/class work

❑ Designing curriculum

❑ Reader's advisory

❑ I do not utilize or borrow materials from the library

❑ Other (please specify): _____

5. I find the library web page helpful.

❑ Strongly agree   ❑ Agree   ❑ Disagree

❑ Strongly disagree   ❑ Don't know

❑ Other (please specify): _____

6. The library has adequate material to support my cur-
    riculum.
    ❏ Strongly agree   ❏ Agree   ❏ Disagree
    ❏ Strongly disagree   ❏ Don't know
    ❏ Other (please specify): _____

7. I am aware of what services the library has to offer.
    ❏ Strongly agree   ❏ Agree   ❏ Disagree
    ❏ Strongly disagree   ❏ Don't know
    ❏ Other (please specify): _____

8. The library is an important part of the school culture.
    ❏ Strongly agree   ❏ Agree   ❏ Disagree
    ❏ Strongly disagree   ❏ Don't know
    ❏ Other (please specify): _____

9. Materials I would like to see added to the collection:

    _____

10. Do you have any other comments or thoughts you would
    like to share?

    _____

Used with permission from the Westborough Public School District.
Please contact Anita Cellucci for further permission if interested in using.
www.surveymonkey.com/s/CXT39PN.

Appendix H

Sample Survey Results for Analysis

The figures below are the hypothetical results of a middle school library student survey question. This is not a report for distribution, but an example of the process of analysis the administrator of the survey might undergo in order to draw conclusions and determine how to use the results in an advocacy effort.

Survey Question and Results

The library meets my needs for school assignments.

Response	Number of students	Percentage of total responses
Always	101	37.0%
Often	88	32.2%
Sometimes	72	26.4 %
Never	6	2.1%
Don't know	6	2.1%
Total responses: 273		

Optional comments:

- I often can't come on a pass because teachers and classes have reserved all the computers.
- Only one color printer.
- Use the computers but not the books.

- Not enough color printing.
- I always start my big assignments in the library.
- I wouldn't do as well in my classes without the library.
- It's always so busy I can't concentrate.

Analysis

Reason for asking question: Librarian is looking to demonstrate that students use the library and that it makes a positive contribution to their school work.

Meets calculated sample size requirements for a group of 500? Yes.

Responses: The overall trend is positive.

- Temporarily putting aside the "don't know" responses, clustering the "always" and "often" responses shows 189 out of 267, or 71 percent, have a favorable opinion regarding the library's ability to meet their needs.
- Clustering "sometimes" and "never" responses results in 78 out of 267 responses, or 29 percent, that are considered negative.
- Students selecting "don't know" or "never" make up 12 out of 273, or 4 percent of respondents. These are the students who are not getting their needs met by the library for school assignments in any way.
- Clustering "sometimes," "never," and "don't know" responses equals 84 out of 273, or a total of 31 percent of students who are not being adequately served by the library.

Conclusion from responses: The library meets the needs of a strong majority of students, and these results support the reason for asking the question. Even so, 31 percent is a significant number of students who are not satisfied or are unaware of how the library can meet their needs.

Optional comments: Examining the comments reveals a few trends.

- Four of the seven comments focus on technology—computer availability and the need for access to color printing.
- Two comments refer to the busyness of the library.
- Two comments are testaments to positive associations with the library and how it meets student needs for assignments.

Conclusion from optional comments: There is a need for greater access to technology in the library, including computers and color printers. The library has a capacity issue: it is clearly being used, but it is at times unavailable to some who wish to use it. Some students are very happy with their library experience in meeting their needs for assignments.

Next steps:

- Try to determine why almost a third of students are not receiving an adequate experience by following up with a targeted survey or focus group.
- Explore as a possible advocacy objective increasing access to technology with more computers, or exploring alternatives such as iPads or a "bring your own device" policy so more students can conduct work through Wi-Fi.

- Explore the possibility of increasing capacity through staffing, resources, or policy changes so that all students who need to use the library can do so.
- Be sensitive to the needs of students who require a less stimulating environment.

This one question has identified multiple needs. It would be virtually impossible to tackle every need identified. Following up to gain more insight, matching needs to objectives that have a realistic chance of success, and matching the objective with a decision maker or funder's priorities will help shape the advocacy effort.

Bibliography

AAPOR Cell Phone Task Force. *New Considerations for Survey Researchers When Planning and Conducting RDD Telephone Surveys in the U.S. with Respondents Reached via Cell Phone Numbers.* American Association for Public Opinion Research, 2010. www.aapor.org/Content/aapor/AdvocacyandInitiatives/Reports/CellPhoneTaskForceReport/.

American Association for Public Opinion Research. "Best Practices for Survey Research." Accessed January 17, 2013. www.aapor.org/Best_Practices1.htm.

———. "Is Survey Research Covered by the Do Not Call Rules?" Accessed January 14, 2013. www.aapor.org/Is_Survey_Research_Covered_by_the_Do_Not_Call_Rules_1.htm.

Anawis, Mark. "Carefully Orchestrated Duet Aids Decisions: Achieving the Right Balance Between Graphics and Statistical Analysis." *Scientific Computing* 28 (January–February 2011): 27–29. General OneFile.

Atkinson, William. "Keep the Customer Satisfied . . . and Engaged: Ten Tips to Forming a Customer Advisory Council." *EHS Today* 4 (July 2011): pp. F–G. General OneFile.

Becker, Karen. "Are You Hearing Voices?" *Quality Progress* 38 (2005): 28–35. ProQuest Platinum.

Bishop, Kay, and Sandra Hughes-Hassell. "Using Focus Group Interviews to Improve Library Services for Youth." *Teacher Librarian* 32 (October 2004): 8–12. Educators Reference Complete.

Bronee, Rueben. "Writing That Counts: Three Ways to Use Numbers Creatively to Communicate." *ContentWise*, January 2009. www.becontentwise.com/Article.php?art_num=5109.

Cope, Meghan. "Interviewing." In *Encyclopedia of Human Geography*, edited by Barney Warf. Thousand Oaks, CA: SAGE, 2006. Gale Virtual Reference Library.

Cox, James, and Keni Brayton Cox. *Your Opinion, Please! How to Build the Best Questionnaires in the Field of Education.* 2nd ed. Thousand Oaks, CA: Corwin Press, 2008.

Czaja, Ronald, and Johnny Blair. *Designing Surveys: A Guide to Decisions and Procedures.* 2nd ed. Thousand Oaks, CA: Pine Forge Press, 2005.

Dillman, Don A., Jolene D. Smyth, and Leah Melani Christian. *Internet, Mail, and Mixed-Mode Surveys: The Tailored Design Method.* 3rd ed. Hoboken, NJ: Wiley & Sons, 2009.

Dubreuil, Chris. "Greater Insight: The Online Dimension." *Marketing*, July 28, 2010, 13. General OneFile.

Dutton, Kevin. *Split-Second Persuasion: The Ancient Art & New Science of Changing Minds.* Boston: Houghton Mifflin Harcourt, 2010.

Farmer, Lesley S. J. "Marketing Principles: School Libraries and Beyond." In *Marketing Your Library: Tips and Tools That Work*, edited by Carol Smallwood, Vera Gubnitskaia, and Kerol Harrod, 32–38. Jefferson, NC: McFarland, 2012.

"Focus Groups." In *Encyclopedia of Small Business*, 3rd ed. Detroit: Gale, 2007. Educators Reference Complete.

Gilmore-See, Janice. *Simply Indispensable: An Action Guide for School Librarians.* Santa Barbara, CA: Libraries Unlimited, 2010.

Gray, Dave. "What Is an Infographic?" *Communication Nation* (blog). November 11, 2007. http://communicationnation.blogspot.com/2007/04/what-is-infographic.html.

Hand, David J. *Statistics: A Brief Insight.* New York: Sterling, 2008.

Holland, Adam. "The Stat Factor." *Library Journal* 133 (August 1, 2008): 50. General OneFile.

Jackob, Nikolaus, Thomas Roessing, and Thomas Petersen. "The Effects of Verbal and Nonverbal Elements in Persuasive Communication: Findings from Two Multi-Method Experiments." *Communications: The European Journal of Communication Research* 36 (2011): 245–71. Academic OneFile.

Krum, Randy. "10 Tips for Designing Infographics." *Digital News Gathering,* April 24, 2010. http://digitalnewsgathering.wordpress.com/2010/04/24/10-tips-for-designing-infographics/.

McCandless, David. "David McCandless: The Beauty of Data Visualization." Ted Conferences, 2010. www.ted.com/talks/lang/en/david_mccandless_the_beauty_of_data_visualization.html.

McNamara, Carter. "Basics of Conducting Focus Groups." Free Management Library. Accessed February 4, 2012. http://managementhelp.org/businessresearch/focus-groups.htm.

National Institute on Aging and National Institute of Child Health and Human Development. *Diverse Voices: The Inclusion of Language-Minority Populations in National Studies: Challenges and Opportunities.* Edited by Rose Maria Li, Peggy McCardle, Rebecca L. Clark, Kevin Kinsella, and Daniel Berch. Bethesda, MD: 2001. www.nichd.nih.gov/publications/pubs/upload/Diverse_Voices.pdf.

Nelson, Sandra. "Library Communication." In *The PLA Reader for Public Library Directors and Managers,* edited by Kathleen M. Hughes, 163–79. New York: Neal-Schuman, 2009.

——. "Presenting Data." In Hughes, *The PLA Reader*, 205–16.

Petersen, Gloria. *The Art of Professional Connections: Seven Steps to Impressive Greetings and Confident Interactions*. Tucson, AZ: Wheatmark, 2011.

Reichertz, Jo. "Communicative Power Is Power over Identity." *Communications: The European Journal of Communication Research* 36 (2011): 147–68. Academic OneFile.

Robbins, Naomi. "How to Exaggerate Trends in Graphs." *Effective Graphs* (blog), September 12, 2012. http://blogs.forbes.com/naomirobbins/2012/09/12/misleading-by-changing-the-aspect-ratio-to-hide-variation-or-exaggerate-trends-in-graphs/.

Ross, Margaret E. "Surveys and Survey Results." In *Encyclopedia of Educational Leadership and Administration*, edited by Fenwick W. English, 984–86. Thousand Oaks, CA: SAGE, 2006. Gale Virtual Reference Library.

"School Libraries Count!" American Association of School Librarians, 2012. www.ala.org/aasl/researchandstatistics/slcsurvey/slcsurvey.

Shelley, Mack C. "Questionnaires." In *Encyclopedia of Educational Leadership and Administration*, edited by Fenwick W. English, 842–46. Thousand Oaks, CA: SAGE, 2006. Gale Virtual Reference Library.

Smiciklas, Mark. *The Power of Infographics: Using Pictures to Communicate and Connect with Your Audiences*. Indianapolis: Que, 2012. Kindle e-book.

Stewart, David W., Prem N. Shamdasani, and Dennis W. Rook. *Focus Groups: Theory and Practice*. 2nd ed. Thousand Oaks, CA: SAGE, 2007.

"Target Audience Planning for All Frontline Advocacy Staff." American Library Association. Accessed January 21, 2103. www.ala .org/advocacy/advleg/advocacyuniversity/frontline_advocacy/ frontline_public/goingdeeper/audienceplanning.

"Toulmin's Argument Model." *ChangingMinds.org*. Accessed January 11, 2103. http://changingminds.org/disciplines/argument/ making_argument/toulmin.htm.

Wanamaker, Karen J. "Flaunt It If You've Got It!" In *Marketing Your Library: Tips and Tools That Work*, edited by Carol Smallwood, Vera Gubnitskaia, and Kerol Harrod, 107–8. Jefferson, NC: McFarland, 2012.

Warren, John T., and Deanna L. Fassett. *Communication: A Critical/Cultural Introduction*. Los Angeles: SAGE, 2011.

Weyland, Mathias. "The Wise Use of Statistics in a Library-Oriented Environment." *Code4Lib Journal* 6 (March 2009). http://journal .code4lib.org/articles/1275.

Wiggins, Grant, and Jay McTighe. *Understanding by Design*. 2d ed. Alexandria, VA: Association for Supervision and Curriculum Development, 2005. Gale Virtual Reference Library e-book.

Williams, Alicia, and Nancy Protheroe. *How to Conduct Survey Research: A Guide for Schools*. Alexandria, VA: Educational Research Service, 2008.

Williams, Robin. *The Non-Designer's Presentation Book*. Berkeley, CA: Peachpit Press, 2010.

Wong, Dona M. *The Wall Street Journal Guide to Information Graphics: The Dos and Don'ts of Presenting Data, Facts, and Figures*. New York: W. W. Norton, 2010.

Yau, Nathan. *Visualize This: The FlowingData Guide to Design, Visualization, and Statistics*. Indianapolis: Wiley, 2011.

Index